Baggage:
Healing from a
Father's Rejection

Trish Russell

DEDICATION

To all my sister friends who have felt the sting of rejection, you are not alone and you are so very loved. So very treasured. And beautiful.

CONTENTS

Introduction

INTRODUCTION

"For I know the plans I have for you," declares the Lord, "plans to prosper you and not to harm you, plans to give you hope and a future." —Jeremiah 29:11 (NIV)

Author's Note: During our time together, I will focus on the significance of our fathers, and the impact they have on the other relationships in our lives. I want to explore why the pain fathers inflict on us runs so deep, why it is necessary not to stuff any rejection away, and *why* the pain is there. Rejection comes in various forms, from emotional to physical absence and from abuse to misuse. As we walk this journey together, I have tried only to focus on what I know personally. This does not mean your pain or personal journey is less significant. My prayer is that you will be able to connect with a piece of my rejection and find your own hope to heal.

As my pain was revealed to me, I kept wondering why it mattered. After all, my mom loves me greatly, and I have wonderful people in my life who care for me. So, why does my father's rejection cut so deep and impact so many different areas of my world? I came to the realization that our fathers are supposed to be an integral part of our lives, and we are meant to look to them to show us how to approach the world. I will rarely mention the role of any other adult in our lives because this book is designed to unpack the baggage of a father's rejection and introduce you to a Father who is waiting to share your life and has loved you through all your struggles.

1

A True Father

No, in all these things we are more than conquerors through him who loved us. For I am sure that neither death nor life, nor angels nor rulers, nor things present nor things to come, nor powers, nor height nor depth, nor anything else in all creation, will be able to separate us from the love of God in Christ Jesus our Lord.
—Romans 8:37-39 (NIV)

I remember the day vividly. My little sister and I were visiting our dad for a few weeks that summer—the only time we would see him all year. I was twelve years old and staring up at the man who had given me life. Without him I would not exist; the sun could rise and set on him if he would just love me. As I stared at him, I knew all my hopes and dreams rested in this moment. I had spent days, weeks, and months building up to this question, silently pleading to be seen and heard...*and loved*. Finally, I gathered my courage and asked the question that had been haunting me.

"Why can't you take time off when we visit?" Ok. I could breathe a little. In a moment there would be no more wondering.

"I did," he responded matter-of-factly.

I was dumbfounded. This was not the response I had expected. I knew most people received a week or two off a year, and this was the only time he would have with my sister and me. Wouldn't he want to soak up every moment with his daughters? Wouldn't he want to spend as much time with us as possible?

"One or two days doesn't count for the whole year," I reasoned.

"I took time off." His voice was firm, hard.

"But we are here for two weeks. You can take off more time." I felt anger and pain rising in me.

"I told you—I took time off," he replied with an elevated firmness as he turned and headed for the kitchen.

"We are your daughters. You don't see us the rest of the year. You should take off more time like other dads," I argued, following him.

"Why are you pushing this?"

"Because other dads take off time. Don't you want to spend time with us?"

"I didn't ask to be your dad. This is who I am. I'm not going to change."

Silence. And in that silence, I crumbled. Gone were the hopes of regular phone calls, summer trips, and days spent playing outside with my dad. Gone were the dreams of relationship.

I don't believe my dad ever expected the situation to unfold like it did. He was the type of man who wants a family without any of the work, the convenience of companionship without actual attachment to the humans living under his roof. It took me over a decade to understand the truth that he was incapable of giving me more than he already did. He sent money and provided food and clothing when we visited, which was a lot more than he had growing up. Unfortunately, this knowledge has not helped me to heal fully. It takes a conscious effort to forgive him every time the wounds are reopened. When he said he did not ask to be my father, I shattered. There was no repairing what happened that day. Some words can never be unheard.

That day he showed me how easy it is to walk out. He felt no obligation to stick around and be part of a family. When he laid out the options and what I saw was less than what my little girl heart desired, I walked out on him. Literally. Again, I'm not sure he ever meant for things to go the way they did because, in his own selfish way, he does love me. In a tiny box with limited contact and no expectations, he loves me. The only piece of his story I'm familiar with is that he grew up in poverty and worked extremely hard for everything he got. I do not fault him for his lack of ability to connect with another human. And maybe, just maybe, if he had never said out loud that he did not want to be my father and did not sign up for the job, reconciliation could have temporarily happened. However, with those words he declared his priorities. I left and rarely looked back.

Have you ever fought hard for something and failed to receive it? Did you craft your argument, plan out the work to achieve a goal, and then, in the end, find you were only left with broken pieces to pick up? Standing up for myself and choosing a different path was only the first step in healing and finding a life of joy. Though I did not know it then, a wound was made that day which would continue to reopen for the rest of my life—that is, until I decided to invite the unconditional Source of love into my heart.

Your situation may not be as dramatic as an ultimatum laid out to you at the tender age of twelve years old; it could be one full of subtle rejection or one of complete absence. Whether you have uncertain pain from your father or vivid memories of hurt, this book is for you.

During our time together, I will share with you the journey I went on to discover a Father's unconditional love for His chosen daughter and show you how I have unpacked the pile of baggage sitting on my doorstep. Some moments are more painful than others. There are years that are darker than I like to admit, but I hope you come to discover that this relationship I have found is available to you as well. The Father I talk about and share with you is not my earthly father; instead, He is the Creator of the Universe, who wants to be invited into a relationship with you and share in your story. He delights in you, and after our time together, I hope you will see how His love allows us to trust the people in our lives, to trust our own judgment, and, ultimately, to trust the words, "You are chosen, made on purpose, and a daughter of Christ."

The heart of the book

My intention for this book is to create a safe place for women to give a voice to the wounds of their past without fear of judgment and without fear of being misunderstood or placated with well-meaning words from loved ones. A father's rejection cuts deep in a way that can be difficult to articulate. Due to the severity of the pain, we tend to lock it away, pushing the hurts out of our hearts and minds. I spent the better part of a decade believing my pain was gone and never wanting to look back because I truly believe it is important to "live in the moment" and enjoy our surroundings. However, as I began to have a family—as the most intimate relationships I would know as an adult grew—I discovered the philosophies of "live for today" and "the past is the past" had become Band-Aids hiding my wounds. Mantras, self-help words, and affirmations are useful, but these methods only work for a short time when we have soul-deep wounds crying out for our attention.

When we take time to look at the pain and sit in a safe place with the past, it does not have to be a dark, all-consuming experience. I shied away from facing my wounds because it was too painful and because I would allow the rejection to creep into my everyday thoughts and actions, so I stuffed my emotions and memories. What I want to share is that, while those difficult days were less than ideal, the choice to walk away from the pain and not acknowledge it brought on days of destruction and soul-wrenching choices. I'm here to share with you a truth: we *can* heal and grow stronger as we unpack our baggage, and this is possible by entering into a loving and healing relationship—but more on that later.

I do want to add a disclaimer up front: by focusing on the pain of a father's rejection, I do not mean to overlook the other intricacies of life. Our lives and personal inner workings are quite complex. It is not just a father's rejection that leads to depression, heartbreaking decisions, volatile parenting, broken marriages, the inability to connect with others, or the absence of unconditional love in our most important relationships. During my life's journey, including a deployment to Afghanistan and a diagnosis of Post Traumatic Stress Disorder (PTSD), I have discovered my father's rejection has been the deepest of wounds and caused the worst damage in my life because I left it buried and unnoticed. The pain was like an overstuffed suitcase ready to pop open at any moment, and once I was married and became a mother, the contents burst open, landing on the dearest people in my world. It took entering into the most intimate relationship of my life for the depths of my pain to be revealed. As I mentioned before, this is not a place we have to stay in. We can move out of the darkness and enter into loving arms.

During my processing of these wounds and their impact on the loved ones around me, I began to wonder if there were other women experiencing this same reality. Are there other women floundering in the midst of battle with unseen demons? Is there a silent war happening in homes around the globe? Are there other daughters who have deep wounds rooted in rejection from the most important man in their life? If so, I am writing to you. In this book, I will focus on how my father's rejection impacted my world in ways that were devastatingly unexpected. Then, I will share the truth, love, and joy that has brought me the greatest healing and peace, even in my darkest moments. Finally, I will offer introductions, thoughts, and ideas for you to bring into your own healing journey.

Here's a startling truth I have come to accept: if you do not know the enemy is lying in wait, if you are not aware of a wound, it can pop out at any time and crumble the world around you. When I returned from Afghanistan, my therapist described my stuffed pain as an overflowing filing cabinet. I had jammed too many memories into one drawer without sorting through them because the content was extremely painful, and I couldn't keep living that way because the past would burst open at the most inopportune times. For the purposes of this book, I have transferred the therapist's analogy of a filing cabinet to suitcases.

My experiences overseas and the type of therapy I received afterwards helped me to identify what was happening when the wounds my father had inflicted came bursting forth. As I tried to navigate the dynamics of being married a handful of years and raising two toddlers and a baby, I fell into a pattern of behavior foreign to me. My response to our family situation revolved around outbursts, mistrust, and insecurity, and I will explore the root of this behavior throughout the book. It took years for me to comprehend the depths of my biological father's rejection and the correlation to how I treated those nearest and dearest to me.

Because of my previous experience with safely unpacking a painful time in my life, I knew there could be a way to navigate my journey to a healthier place when I realized what was happening with the wounds my father left me. In contrast to my PTSD therapy, the moment of clarity and first true steps of healing didn't happen until I invited God into the picture. Before I could do that, however, He had to reveal the truth of my pain, and He revealed it suddenly one day when I was pushing all three of my children on the swings in our backyard. Fortunately, He had been planting many seeds along my journey in order to prepare me so that I wouldn't run away or shut down. In fact, I was relieved. My prayer is that this book is a seed on your journey to discovering a life of healing and redemption.

The one relationship that has proven to be the most important for my healing is the one with my true Father. Through every single up and down, He is by my side, encouraging me to keep moving forward and try again. He is always reassuring me that I am loved, seen, and valued. The popular saying "hindsight is 20/20" is quite applicable here. When I take a moment to look back, I can see Him walking alongside me in darkness and guiding me to the light.

Hearing that God the Almighty, Creator of Heaven and Earth, loves you is one thing. Experiencing that love and receiving it into your heart is an entirely different reality. It has taken me several decades to realize my Father's Love, and, if you'll allow me, I'd like to take you on that journey. Through our time together, my prayer is that you will be able to identify where you are in your relationship with your Father and dare to dream what it could become.

If you do not have any type of relationship with God, I hope you will choose to join in the journey. I believe each person who comes into our path is there for a reason. Maybe this book will allow you to know you are not alone. By nature, I'm a skeptic, and my skepticism often clashes with my eternally optimistic personality, causing some interesting internal battles, but in spite of this, I have found hope and truth for my story. As we walk through these pages together, I invite you to discover hope and truth for yours. Do not take my word for it; this is just one woman's journey on paper. Unpack the truths that resonate with you, and please throw away the ones that don't. One of the most beautiful aspects of our time on earth is that each of us has a unique journey. I would not impose mine on you; however, I will be so bold as to invite you to sit for a while and take a peek into mine in the hopes that it may encourage you in yours. Who knows? Maybe out of our time together you'll discover a new truth and go on to share it with another daughter of Christ wounded by her earthly father.

Meeting God in a new way

Inside each woman is a little girl who yearns to be cherished and wholly accepted for the unique soul she is today and for the person she dreams of becoming tomorrow. The hopes of our innocence are a gift to the world, but through pain, trials, and tribulations, we forget about the innocent little girl inside us. At times, it can be too painful to see her and be reminded of what has not come to be. Sometimes, choosing to keep the door closed seems smarter because it keeps the demons and disappointments at bay.

My dream is for each woman to rediscover the innocent hopes and dreams she had as a child in order to enter into each day the way she was created to live it. The journey to reconnect with that place is quite personal and may take a lifetime to discover. Each of us has a special place in our heart where our hopes and dreams are stored. Some of us have the courage and bravery to open up the secret place and share it with the world. Others leave it locked away, and some have even forgotten that this special place exists.

If you are longing for something more in your life, if you wake up and know you desire more for your relationships and your daily activities, I invite you on a journey. Uncovering the hurts from the past is not easy. Whether your father was an active participant in your life or a biological donor to your existence, your pain is true, real, and valid. Your thoughts, ideas, and perceptions are your truth. While I can't speak into them or anyone else's with accuracy, there is One who can.

Throughout my journey, there is One who has heard each of my hurts, each of my pain points, and has not tried to give me another version of them or to placate me. He has simply listened and waited until I was ready to hear His truths. We have been on a five-year journey together of uncovering the truth, and it wasn't until recently that all the pieces fell into place. He did not rush me, discount my fears or thoughts, or tell me my opinion was skewed by a child's viewpoint. He listened to, waited for, and loved me. When I called, He was there and answered.

Turning our eyes to God when we have had difficulty and struggle is hard; it is not intuitive. It takes habit; it takes consistency, and, for some of us who know God, it takes feeling convicted when we don't choose to turn to Him. So, it's easy for me to say, "Turn to God"; however, I know it's a lot more complicated than scheduling time on the calendar to chat with our Abba (an intimate term used for God as our Father). He also knows this and is not intimidated. Abba is ready to fight for your attention, free you from guilt, and help you make time with Him a habit. He wants to be your "rock" in any situation (see Psalm 18:2), no matter how long it has been since you reached out to Him and even if you have never invited Him in.

Now that you know there is no expectation for you to have it all together and get it right the first, second, or millionth time, what's next? How do you turn back to God after you've been hurt so badly, your heart is broken, and you are shattered? How do you turn to God if you've heard in church that He is a fierce God? It's hard to believe that a fierce God will tenderly hold you and keep you close. Or, how do you turn to God when you may not even know who He is? You've been told that God exists and that you must love Him, follow Him, and obey Him, but you've never actually met Him. Or, your perception of God may be that He is controlling. How do you turn to Him then? And how do you invite God in when you *have* turned to Him, shared life with Him, and trusted Him, only to have what you specifically prayed for not come to fruition? How do you turn to God in the messiness and the pain? How do you turn when you want to run away? There are many reasons we hesitate to bring our wants, needs, and desires to His feet, and it can be even harder for us to think about bringing our deepest wounds and insecurities. How do we turn to a God we haven't come to understand? How do we trust Him?

I'd like us to unpack these questions and discover answers together. It is not an easy journey, but neither is life in our world. A relationship with God is not intended to give us warm, fuzzy feelings. It is intended to fill the gaping hole inside of us that we cannot fill with worldly things no matter how hard we try—even good things like a loving relationship, a good job, or constant volunteer work. This hole remains no matter how many people we serve or how many years we spend seeking the love of people. The hole remains. It still hurts, and the baggage of our past rejections is waiting to jump out and unleash its hurt and pain on the ones around us unless we continue to internalize it all. However, when our hole is healed and filled with God's mercy and grace, He can change our story and make us into the people we were created to be. We need Him in order for this change to occur. It is incredibly difficult to live life with abandon and full openness when we do not trust, when we are wary of those around us, and when we constantly leave a part of ourselves locked away.

I have discovered God is a safe place to turn to. Through my relationship with Him, I am shown mercy and grace as I battle demons and wrestle with haunting memories. He shows me there is another way to live and approach each day and the relationships in my life.

Many people discuss the importance of forgiveness in order to heal and move on from the past. I agree. In this book I would like to add to the conversation. Through my experience of growing my own family unit, I abruptly discovered there were some pieces missing for me to be a loving wife and mother. Through my relationship with my True Father, I learned to fully trust myself and those around me because He consistently showers me with mercy, grace, and unconditional love.

I'm not going to placate you with pleasantries. Through our time together, I will share my darkest moments and how I fought to pull out of them. In each chapter the tools I used to forge a new path for my family and life will be laid out. My prayer is that you will walk away knowing your future is not written in stone and the past can be washed away. You are worthy of greatness, love, and happiness.

Journal Prompt

A healthy way to process information is by writing down our thoughts and emotions. Throughout our time together, I will share writing prompts and prayers to guide you in this. These journal prompts are an opportunity to begin inviting God into the conversation.

1) As you read this chapter, what emotions did you feel?

2) What role did your biological father have in your life?

3) What is the nature of your current relationship with the man you consider to be your father?

4) Why did you pick up this book?

5) How do you want this book to impact your life?

Prayer

Dear Father, please be with me during this journey as I uncover my past and bring my wounds to Your feet. Shield me from distractions and temptations to run away from the true pain of rejection, and, instead, help me to find courage and strength in You as I seek healing and love. Please show me Your grace and mercy in safe places so that I may know You more and trust the truth of Your promises. Thank You for the blessings of my life, the opportunity to know You more and not be chained to my past, and the promise of a new life in You. Amen.

2

Friendships

Therefore encourage one another and build one another up, just as you are doing. – 1 Thessalonians 5:11 (ESV)

Adolescence was brutal. Not "long day at the office, I need a glass of wine" brutal, but knocked-down, dragged-out brutal. There may be a small group of people on this planet who did not suffer or experience extreme awkwardness during middle school and high school. I am unable relate to those people because I was quirky, uncomfortable, and painfully insecure. I believe most of us felt out of sorts and self-conscious during those difficult years, but some of us were able to hide it better than others.

Within those years of hormonal growth, there are bound to be a few moments here and there that bring extreme mortification. Mine happened at an early stage in the adolescent journey. I'll never forget the day the world showed me the harshness of teenage friendship. I sat at the cafeteria table and believed it was any other day of teenage oddness, juggling too many textbooks in my backpack and navigating crushes and weekend plans. As I sat with the only friends I had, I heard the words every insecure and awkward girl fears: "We don't want to be your friends anymore."

I was stunned. Shocked. There was no reason given. I had not committed some major grievance by posting an embarrassing picture to Facebook. (We didn't even have the internet back then.) There was no stolen boyfriend. None of the girl codes had been broken. As I sat wondering why the only three people I knew chose not to be my friends anymore, my heart was shattered. What had I done? What was wrong with me? Now what? Literally. *Now what?*

I rode thirty minutes home to the military base with these girls. There was nowhere for me to hide. All the while I was thinking, *How will I find new friends?* These were the only three girls in my grade on the base, and it was not commonplace to cross grades and age gaps during those treacherous adolescent years.

Sometimes I wonder if this is why I pushed my biological father to tell me he loved me. Sixth grade was horrible. I had just moved to a new base and didn't know anyone. We were thirty minutes away from the locals on a mountain, and there was no mingling with the people who lived in town—at least not when you were twelve and didn't have a car. There was no participating in community activities; it was too far away, and the base provided few opportunities. We were isolated, and my only friends had just unceremoniously ditched me.

By the end of the school year, two of the girls had apologized and asked to be my friends again. Of course, I was open to that because, again, twelve-year-old adolescence is painfully lonely. Also, I had conquered as many levels as I could on Nintendo's Super Mario Brothers and wasn't keen to try new games. I just wanted friends and a regular GPA.

Have you ever had a horrible friend moment—one that leaves you perplexed and devastated? Maybe you are currently working hard to discover how to navigate a new relational dynamic. Relationships are always more difficult in real life than in the movies, at least in the movies I grew up watching, which always ended with apologies and restored friendships.

Relationships are full of complications and layered emotions, even for adults. If you add in adolescent hormones and life transitions, feelings will inevitably be hurt, and insecurities will develop. After a rough year in a new school, I felt driven to make some changes in my world and redefine some relationships. (I am a firstborn child, after all.) As I went to spend two weeks with my biological father that summer, I prepared for the talk I had planned. I couldn't continue in what he defined as a "father-daughter" relationship anymore.

This was when I had the conversation with my father that I shared at the beginning of the book. I wanted to know... Why did he work the whole time? Why didn't he send us cards? Why didn't he talk to me about anything beyond birth control and my weight?

As you already know, my attempt to fight for a life-giving relationship was not well received.

When we have devastating situations happen in our lives or multiple rejections back-to-back, either we surrender to unhealthy desires to please others and fit in, or we rebel. Yes, I know. Rebellion and people-pleasing can be normal responses to the challenges of growing up. I have come to discover that while these are normal, we make decisions out of our pain that stay with us for a lifetime. Those decisions shape our identities, and we take those identities with us as we grow up. Then, we fall into patterns of behavior without knowing where the root of them lies. This unawareness can make it difficult to leave an abusive relationship, trust girlfriends, or set healthy boundaries.

Personally, I went into a year of people-pleasing and trying to fit in. As I entered another year of middle school with one of my parents out of the picture and my only two friends questionable, I didn't have a lot of hope. What does friendship look like after rejection? Not healthy, to say the least. Pretty soon, I entered a rebellious phase.

In order to fit in, I experimented with boys and smoked pot (once). Yeah. Not my proudest moments. I'm a quick study, though. I decided the pot scene was a waste of time. I didn't see the point in taking a drug that led merely to a really good giggle session with friends. The two boy situations were the result of trying to fit in mixed with the baggage from a non-existent father-daughter relationship. So those adolescent decisions were a combination of multiple insecurities that had at their root a desire to be loved and accepted. Even though I did not want to be alone, my few attempts to fit in left me feeling uncomfortable and sick to my stomach, so I chose to walk away from those friends.

Even when you choose to forge a new path for yourself, how do you move forward from mess-ups, mistakes, and poor choices? One step at a time. Seriously. Some of those days continued to haunt me until my thirties and triggered a pattern of behavior that would become my default in my mid-twenties.

I was able to finish middle school and high school with a seemingly normal routine and experience. During those years, we moved to the town where the schools were, and I was finally able to breathe. Things weren't perfect, though. As a military kid, you are always on the outs of a small town, but, then again, during those years who isn't out of place and trying to survive?

While my year of rebellion positively impacted my response to future social pressures in middle and high school, the awkwardness of making friends never went away. However, as I grew up, I developed a knack for connecting with people in a variety of social groups and bridging the gap of differences to discover common interests. I fine-tuned the skill of avoiding social situations but appearing engaged when I received my driver's license. Instead of hanging out with friends on the weekend, I would work, and I continued this habit through college.

Instead of facing my fears of friendships and rejection, which I'm not sure how you do in a healthy way during the years of "raging hormones," I made use of my time to lead a productive, fruitful life. As I socialized in very controlled situations with little commitment to be transparent and vulnerable, I was able to continue connecting with people, but a hole remained. Even though I participated in clubs and organizations, attended school dances, and made the occasional appearance at get-togethers, my circle of friends was incredibly limited. This life skill of self-protection has carried over into adulthood.

I'm a freakishly introspective person, but this might be your first time exploring the impact of your father's rejection on your friendships. I'll gently ask some prompting questions now to get the wheels turning before we move on to discuss how to process the pain and find mercy and grace in those difficult moments.

Reflective questions about friendship:
Are you satisfied with how you interact with your friends?
Do you have two or three close friends you can trust with any thought or idea?
Have you laughed with a friend in the last six months?

If you answered "yes" to all those questions, then you are probably well-adjusted in the area friendship. Our wounds can surface in different areas of our lives but not necessarily all of them, like I originally thought. For example, I used to think there was something wrong with my quirky way of socializing. Through God's healing, I've come to discover that the ways I adapted were natural for my personality and were heightened during the years I tried to forge ahead on my own without Him.

If you answered any of those questions with "no," I would encourage you to think about the root of your answer. Is there a character trait or response in friendship you long to possess but do not have yet? Yes, I do believe you can cultivate the traits you desire. We can learn behaviors, skills, and mindsets in order to become the best version of ourselves. It takes work and discipline, but it is possible!

So, how have you adapted? When our fathers reject us, something inside us breaks. If you claim not to be broken or hurt in some way, then my question to you is, have you healed through counseling or redemption? Or, are you like I was—living in pain without knowing it? The main reason we break is that one of our key relationships, one we should be able to rely on for support and consistency, doesn't exist the way we long for it to, and there is a ripple effect to that kind of pain. We may lose the ability to trust. Others' fickleness can cut so deep that we become hesitant to allow new people in. Sometimes we overthink how we respond in certain situations, become extreme people pleasers, or become reclusive. Navigating this world is difficult enough, and when a pile of rejection is added, it's a miracle we have any healthy relationships at all. If you don't have a single life-giving relationship, there is good news. You can.

My year of rebellion was a gift because it helped me become able to identify the kind of friends I wanted to surround myself with, rather than fall into the social norm to fit in. As an adult, this has led to my desire and ability to truly care for others, no matter the distance, and to be able to pick up old friendships where they left off.

Hope

There is a song I wish I had heard as an adolescent. Fortunately, I hear it often now, and I dance in the kitchen when I do, waving my hands in the air "like I just don't care." The song is called "The God I Know," and it speaks to all the pieces of a young girl navigating the hallways of friendship. The band sings about trying to fit in, working hard to be good enough, and always falling short of all the expectations thrown upon us in life. Then a miracle happens, someone loves me for me, no strings attached, and exactly the way I am.

The first time I heard this song, I thought the writers were referencing the struggles of a young Christian navigating the church world and trying to understand how to balance the expectations of their parents and environment. However, after a few listens, I realized these words reminded me of what it felt like going to school each day, fitting in at social events, and navigating the entire adolescent experience. I was always trying to fit in, be the perfect teenage girl, and be accepted by others—until my junior year.

By the time I was a junior, I was sick and tired of trying to play the game and fit in with those around me. I felt wearied by the constant fear of rejection and the battle with those emotions when they came to the surface. We were all in survival mode during middle and high school; there were hurt feelings and casualties of character on all sides.

What I love about the song I just quoted, which was only released in 2016, is that it gives my rebellious, awkward self a new way to remember those years, a healing of sorts. During our adolescence, we are faced with peer and family pressure to act a certain way and live up to the expectations of others. Acceptance hinders our ability to fulfill the role others have cast us in. The person of our youth is rarely the adult of our present. If we don't give ourselves permission to release the roles of the past and grow into the person we were created to be, healthy friendships may continue to be a struggle.

Growing up, we are given a vision of friendship through the lens of our environment. Maybe you learned about friendships from television or in books. Your parents may have taught you the intricacies of interpersonal relationships. All of these can be good resources for relational learning and growth. Yes, you read that correctly. Television can be a quality resource when used properly. It gave me a window to pop culture, how popular kids interacted with one another, and some of the nuances in relationships.

We have these different avenues of discovering relationships, and if you have children, this how they are learning along with what you share. The piece I loved discovering—the one that ended up opening a whole new world for me—is that God is part of friendship, too. I had no idea God was even interested in friendships. I kept Him in a box. I spent time with Him on Sundays and did my best to honor His commandments throughout the week, but that was it. Why would the God of the universe have any interest in my friendships? This truth is something I am still learning to apply in my life by inviting Him into the relationships around me.

The concept of God as a friend was introduced to me my senior year of college with this Phillips, Craig & Dean song, "A Friend of God." Entering into a relationship as a friend with the Lord was a very radical idea. At the time I am sure it shook up a lot of congregations. As a Catholic girl we were encouraged to reverently look upon the cross, keeping the Holiness of the Lord far away from us mere mortals.

I remember attending a Phillips, Craig and Dean concert at a good ole Southern Baptist Church. It was so moving that I stood and worshipped openly for one of the first times in my life. Afterward, my very conservative fiancé shared that I had inspired his sister to be able to worship God because if someone like me could worship God and accept Him as a friend, then anyone could. To be honest, I have no idea what that statement meant. I was a 22-year-old virgin who didn't drink alcohol. My relationship with Christ was somewhat new, but I had been raised a good Catholic girl who respected the Almighty. I share this moment because people are strange. When you are in relationships with others, they will say things that don't make sense and can even be hurtful. That's where God comes in. Rather than being offended, I chose to focus on the fact that my love of hearing that God wants to be my friend had moved another person in her walk. If I had not been focused on that at the time, my reaction could have been very different.

How many times have you been in conversation with someone and their words hit you the wrong way? In those situations, I tend to shut down to prevent myself from saying something I will regret. Other times, I allow my words to fly, and there's no holding back. When the latter happens, my words can either come from a place of grace and understanding or from a place of bitterness and hurt. Knowing how to move forward and invest in the relationship can be difficult when conflict arises. This is where my reliance on God has been really helpful with friendships.

Since God wants to be my friend, He shows me how to be one to others. I no longer try to discover why an awkward situation happened or if my time with this person is for a "season, reason, or lifetime." God is there with me, talking to me, and allowing me to lean on His expertise because here's the thing: He has insider information I am not privy to. God knows the home environment of my friend, the mental or emotional struggles she may be going through, and more. When I invite God into my friendships, whether the other person knows it or not, He's my helper. No longer am I relying on my own emotions, perceptions, and thoughts. And, let me tell you, this has been a great relief! People are so dynamic that it would take me a week (or more) to figure out if my friend was happy, mad, or sad. As a busy mama of three littles invested in her marriage, that is too much work. If I had to do all of that on my own, I would give up on the friendship, continue to overthink, or become defensive. Instead, with God at the center of my relationships, if a weird moment happens with a friend, I give it to Him. There is always a little analysis of the situation—I just can't help it. I'm wired to be an analyst. However, I am able to release the confusion or struggle to Him. The blessing I have seen come out of this is my ability to respond to friends after difficult situations. Instead of being leery or grounded in defensive thoughts and emotions, I'm able to enter conversations with an open mind and release the past. One of my philosophies is, "If someone has an issue or concern and doesn't say anything, then it isn't real. I'm available and ready if there is a topic necessary to discuss." This attitude has allowed me to free up a lot of mental and emotional energy surrounding friendships.

What would it feel like to walk away from an awkward situation knowing you had a reliable source to vent to—Someone who was going to listen and guide you in the right next steps, not drum up more drama and anxiety over a conversation or misunderstanding? No matter what you have done in life, there is one Friend who will always be there for you and will guide you in each relationship. Man! Having an insider like God in your relationships is better than having the NSA for topography analysis!

While the little girl who was rejected lives inside of you, she can be guided, shown a new path, and begin to heal. She no longer has to sit on the side of her bed, weeping and wishing for acceptance. She can be seen and heard today through your actions. Sitting with your past wounds is quite uncomfortable, even painful. I do not enjoy revisiting that lunchroom table and its aftermath. That's a place in my past I prefer to keep right where I left it, but I've discovered that it continues to pop up in different areas of my life because that little girl sitting at the table being rejected needs me to see her. There was no daddy-hero waiting at home to pick her up from the heart shattering rejection and remind her she's loved, special, and beautiful. This little girl is desperate for someone to come alongside her and say, "I know this hurts. I am so sorry this is painful. You did nothing wrong. You are loved and cared for," and then wrap her in a loving embrace that she knows is from someone who sees her, knows her, and will continue to care for her.

I am not able to do this on my own, though. It is through the love and mercy of God that I am able to pick up that little girl and rock her in my lap because He is holding me and rocking me in His. She needs me to hold her, speak life over her, share the truth of her beauty, and encourage her tender heart. Her future self requires this of me because when the "friends" rejected the little girl, they reaffirmed all the horrible things her earthly father had said, and their actions mimicked his. If he didn't want her, who could? The affirmation of a father's rejection through friendship can be crippling. It would be nice to believe that the doubts and fears about friendship go away as we get older; however, when wounds are left untended, they can fester. The lie, "Why put yourself out there again when your mom is the only person on this planet who seems to like you?" may be alive in your subconscious, impacting relationships and the ability to connect without you realizing it. There is hope. That lie can be quieted and replaced with truth.

Through God's love and mercy, the hurts you have felt through rejection can be healed. You can hug the little girl inside you and be led by God's love to keep taking steps forward. I won't lie; in the beginning it is painful to grow out of the rejection. We are wired for self-preservation. Why would we willingly open a wound and look inside? That sounds horrible! Right? We are fearful of the unknown—of unlocking what lies within. We remember how unpleasant the experience was the first time, so why in the world would we choose to relive the pain? Here's why: if we do not, then we will remain stuck. I know you are longing for a change, or you would not be reading this book. There is good news, friend. You are not on your own.

We find this truth in Psalm 37:23-24: "The Lord makes firm the steps of the one who delights in him; though he may stumble, he will not fall, for the Lord upholds him with his hand." God is ready to hold you as you navigate the uncertainties of friendships and become more vulnerable and open with others.

I never sat still long enough to be rejected.

One way I used to hide from the possibility of rejection was by being too busy. My involvement in clubs and groups fueled my desire for friendship; however, these communities kept me in a bubble. I'm not sure this approach to life was ever a conscious decision; it has been my "MO" since high school, and I never looked back—until I became a mom. As I looked at my little babies, I realized I did not want to miss moments with them by being busy. So, my husband and I decided to keep our world small for the first years of our children's lives.

About the same time, God called me to live differently than those around me. He called me to live as if I was in a village. If someone was sick, I was to bring them food. When another person was having a hard day, I was supposed to stop everything and sit and listen. In the transition to motherhood and in following God's call, I witnessed my life tempo change. No longer was I filling up every hour of the day with extracurricular activities; instead, I was pouring each moment into people.

God was really strategic with His calling because I did not see the change happening in my life until a few years in. I went from being in organizations and protecting myself from relationships to being present for His Church every day. My vulnerabilities in friendship were revealed. I don't blame all my insecurities and quirks on my father's rejection; some of my oddities are due to my own personality. What I have witnessed is an internal shift toward those around me as I rely on God to hold my hand at gatherings and social functions. Anytime my feelings are hurt or I feel misunderstood, I go to Him. I ask Him, *Should I leave or stay? Are these the people You want me to be spending my time with?* And each time, He guides me and gives me strength to push through my pain and awkwardness.

If we have chaotic life tempos, it can be easy to blame our lack of personal engagement on being busy. Now, as a busy mom who is a friend to other busy moms, it is not uncommon for me to find that every person I talk with seems overly busy with life commitments. I wonder what is fueling our busyness. Have you taken a moment to reflect on your willingness to say "yes" to another group or project? Does that willingness come out of a desire to please? Sometimes our motivation to volunteer and sign up is a desire to fit in. This desire is not inherently bad. We are created for community, and being involved in the world around us is good. But we should watch for signs that we are overcommitted because they can indicate a deeper problem. For me, the underlying reason to be busy was a learned defensive position to keep people at arm's length. After all, if you appear to be very social by doing so many good things for others, no one questions why you aren't able to spend time at a dinner or Bible study.

So, if you find yourself overcommitted, let's discover what is fueling your commitments and activities and how you are deciding which friendships to develop. Time in silence and solitude with God has brought answers to my heart. Asking the counsel of trusted friends or loved ones has also helped me as I have tried to discern whether the community I was dedicating my time to was life-giving or soul-sucking. Making space to hear God's whispers over our lives can seem impossible when we are juggling life and family, but it can be done.

How do you decide to make a commitment to a group or friendship? This can be a daunting question because there are so many nuances in the culture we live in today. People are busy and will cancel on you a half-dozen times before you actually connect and see one another. There is the classic, "We should get coffee sometime," or "I'd love to have dinner with you." But then the call never happens. The text goes unanswered. Then, the feelings of rejection set in, and you start to think it's you—maybe you did something wrong. Or you become defensive and put up a wall and choose not to allow anyone else in for a while because the pain of rejection is back and it is too great to put yourself in that situation again. I understand. When the pain of rejection is rooted in a tank-sized case of baggage, it can come rearing its ugly head with a vengeance. Let's take a moment and unpack some of that baggage left on your doorstep, so you can be released to explore friendships.

While we logically know our friend's lack of a response to a text message inviting her to *actually have coffee* probably has nothing to do with us, it still hurts. When those moments happen to me, the little girl sitting in the cafeteria being rejected by her only three friends comes to the surface of my heart again. I feel unsteady, unsure of my footing, and lost for words. Should I text this person again? Do I say "hi" when I see her again? If so, do I ask if she still wants to get together and if she got my text message? Oh, gosh. Maybe I will just stay in my house and never go out again. *Big sigh.* Well, that's not practical. So, what do I do?

Right now, I want you to know that when this happens to you, it **IS** your friend, not you. People are genuinely wrapped up in their lives, consuming information from all sides, and they have forgotten how to stop, sit, and breathe. If they are not in the habit of sitting for longer than a quick meal, then their life rhythm does not allow for coffee dates, catch-ups, and necessary time spent with other humans to develop a basic level of friendship. See. It's not you. It's them.

Don't worry, I'm not going to leave you hanging. There are ways to identify when to continue reaching out, pouring into another person despite the situation, and seeing what may come of the connection. If someone brings a smile to your face and the conversation flows easily between you both, then this is a person to invest in, and it's time to tell the fear of rejection to take a hike.

When the opportunity for coffee or catch-up is nearly impossible, I invest in friends by praying for them, sending them notes in the mail, bringing treats (flowers, coffee) by their house, and sending texts such as, "How are you today? Is there a way I can be praying for you?" Depending on their own season of life, it is quite likely there is no emotional energy to form a new friendship. While the lack of coffee dates can certainly feel like rejection, it could simply be a "not right now" instead. Have you ever been in a season where life is so chaotic you barely have room to breathe, much less get your hair done and take a bubble bath? If there's no room for your favorite things, then it can be excruciatingly painful to make space for another human.

After I look past my feelings of rejection and get out of my own head space, I realize it is ridiculous for me to think I can be friends with all these fabulous people I run into. There's simply not enough hours in the day to stay connected to them and still pour into my family and live in the world as God calls me to. When I sat with that realization for a little while, I then wondered, *Well, what should it be then? How do I know when to pursue a spark in a friendship or allow it to be caught by the wind and pass me by?*

I look to Jesus for direction. Since I strive to live my life as He did His—oh, and fall short at least two minutes after my feet hit the floor in the morning, but, hey, I'm still trying—I look to His friendship circle. How many people did He surround himself with? Who were His people? What did that look like? At first, I was quite inspired when I realized the number was twelve! Ok, that seemed totally doable. I could certainly narrow down my social dreams and aspirations to twelve friends. So, I went and looked at my text message world to see which twelve ladies I had chatted with recently...

Sinking feeling. There weren't twelve. Oh, man! Rejection started to creep in. Then, I looked at Jesus again. He actually only had Peter, James, and John in His inner circle. He surrounded himself with twelve people as His close group of friends, but only three were part of His inner circle. I'll be honest, that was a huge relief when I read that! I started to look at friendship differently, too. There are twelve people in my life that I can call at a moment's notice to say "hi," catch up, and see how they are. I feel comfortable reaching out and seeing how their world is going.

There was something else that happened when I looked at Jesus and His closest friends. I saw disappointment, frustration, let downs, and very human moments. Oh, this was hard to see because if these friends let Jesus down, surely I would be let down, too. Then, these questions crept in -- *What standard am I holding my friendships to? Is it an ideal that does not exist? I mean, if God the Almighty struggled to have friends stay awake and pray for Him during His darkest hour, who am I to expect sainthood from my girlfriends?*

Journal Prompt

When we have been wounded in one area of our life, it can filter into the other parts without us realizing it. When we frame our friendships as Jesus did, then we can begin to heal from the rejections of the past and make room for healthy perspectives and joy.

1) Do you have a healthy friendship in your life? If so, what does it look like?

2) How do you protect yourself from letting others in?

3) When was the last time you felt hurt by a friend's words or actions?

4) Which three words do you want people to think of when they hear your name?

Prayer

God, allow me to see You in the moments of my deepest pain. Help me look back and see You sitting there with me, holding my hand, never letting me go. In the moments when I have felt rejection, when the wound was so deep that it cut through my soul, please show me Your presence. As I move forward and continue to seek You in the healing of my hurts so that I may be able to be used for Your Glory, guide me. Bring people into my world to speak truth over me and encourage me. You know the depths of my heart, and I thank You for Your unending love and grace. In Jesus Name, Amen.

3

Marriage

Be kind to one another, tenderhearted, forgiving one another,
as God in Christ forgave you.
- Ephesians 4:32

I made a fatal mistake. This was never supposed to happen. How could I have been so stupid, not seeing the obvious signs right in front of me? Now I'm stuck. What am I supposed to do next? Counseling? Well, that is out because he said that was not an option. Divorce? We aren't supposed to be together, and I was too dumb to see all the signs.

I grabbed my keys, stormed out of our newlywed apartment, and jumped into my red Dodge Nitro, ready to go anywhere, as long as it was away from him. This man I had committed my life to had no sense or the first clue about how to treat me and cherish me as a wife. Somehow, two years of friendship had not given him the foundation necessary to know the first thing about caring for me.

I drove around my new home, a Midwestern town with no friends or acquaintances to meet and no activities to distract me from the visceral pain in my heart. After I was tired of aimlessly driving around, I ended up at the local bookstore because I'm not a big clothes shopper, which, in hindsight, was a blessing because my emotional turmoil would have racked up a lot of shopping sprees. Now that I was in my safe place, surrounded by nonjudgmental and empathetic books, I desperately looked around for a title to capture my interest and pull me away from my bleak reality. I longed for an opportunity to escape the truth of my marriage and the hopelessness facing me back home.

Eventually, I realized escape wasn't the key. I did not want to hear about someone else's life and the wonderful things taking place in his or her world, fact or fiction. I decided to be proactive. We were married, supposedly blissful newlyweds. Maybe I needed to learn something about being married. With a newfound focus, I desperately looked around the discount section and then the self-help section for a book that would help me understand my personal struggle. I ended up in the Christian books. I'd like to tell you there was one book that changed my marriage and brought us together. It would be wonderful to say, "This was the key to solving all our strife and heartache!" Unfortunately, this step was only the beginning in uncovering the truth of my struggle in our marriage.

During my hours at the bookstore, I battled with my perception of my husband and our marriage. At some point I concluded I had married a man who liked the idea of being married but did not actually act out the role of husband in a kind and loving way, and on the heels of these thoughts, another realization dawned on me. We weren't even six months into our marriage, and I wanted to leave. He probably wanted to leave, too. I assumed he would. And there was no one else I wanted to be with. It was him or a life of missionary work in a foreign land. Little did I know that I was already doing missionary work in a foreign land by being married and building a new family. There had never been a Trish and Kurt Russell before; we had no prior versions of ourselves to reference for clarity and help. At the time this was the worst news ever because I was sure he would leave. I had a deeply rooted belief that if my earthly father could so easily turn his back on me, then there was no hope for anyone else to love me.

It would be another year or so before the truth of my doubts and insecurities came to the surface. I wish I could blame it on all the traveling my husband did in our first year of marriage, on living in a new town, or on my inability to find a job; however, there was a darkness at the root of my insecurities, and it would take going away for the weekend for it to finally be revealed. So, throughout this time I continued to plead with God for revelation and insight on how to be a loving, God-fearing wife.

Have you ever felt this way in your marriage—as though you were in a foreign land, uncertain of your footing and how to communicate with the local population? Bringing two lives together as one can be the most painful experience some of us have ever had. While there are some couples who look into each other's eyes and every little nuance clicks, Kurt and I were polar opposites! Our transition into marriage was more like two tectonic plates of the earth coming together—lots of turmoil, loud noises (shouting), and sharp edges. We both worked and prayed for the end result to be a beautiful, majestic mountain reflecting God's love and glory rather than an unpredictable volcano ready to spew at any moment.

Marriage is a daunting relationship for even the most well-adjusted person, which doesn't really define the majority of us when we start to pull back the layers of our past. So, when the greater adult population is trying to figure out this "'til death do us part" stuff, where do we go for insights and guidance?

Fortunately, we are given a guide in Ephesians that is as applicable today as it was when it was written (60-61 AD), so we can take these words to heart and build our marriages on them. Most Christians are familiar with the verses that discuss how a wife is to submit to her husband, but for the purposes of this book (healing from our fathers' rejection and discovering our Abba's love in order to trust), I would like to highlight a different verse in Ephesians. Before calling on wives to submit to husbands, Paul calls BOTH the husband and the wife to submit. When we are navigating deep wounds and bridging gaps in order to build trust, I believe this verse (Ephesians 5:21) provides a strong foundation for us to build our marriages upon:

> **Submit to one another out of reverence for Christ.**
> **—Ephesians 5:21 (NIV)**

I absolutely love the truth found in this verse and how it reveals the true nature of our Father. Our Abba does not tell us to blindly submit to our husbands; instead, He calls both husband and wife to submit to one another. Our Father wants us to have loving marriages built on Him. Our Creator is the only one strong enough to conquer the complexities of marriage. He is the only one who can see inside our hearts and help us navigate the landmines waiting to jump out during a tense holiday situation or the transition to becoming parents.

The enemy is fully aware of our wounds and the triggers waiting to be pulled that can escalate a simple conversation to World War III. However, when we center our marriage on Christ and each spouse submits to the other out of reverence, we have invited Him into our lives and hearts. He will go before us and make a way. The Lord can go inside our hearts and heal wounds when we allow Him in our world. When we choose to submit to one another out of love for Christ, then we are intentionally choosing a new path. A new way of fighting. A new way of navigating the complexities of marriage and parenthood.

God inspired this Scripture to be worded, "out of reverence for Christ," because He knows we are unable to submit on our own. Whether you are in a relationship with two dominant personalities, two submissive personalities, or a mix, a beautiful harmony takes place when both you and your husband are committed to submitting your wants, needs, and desires to each other "out of reverence for Christ." What does this mean in layman's terms? It means each person takes into consideration the other's day-to-day struggles and long-term dreams, finds ways to support that person, and carves out space and time to connect with and pour into that person, seeing and valuing who that person is. For example, if one partner is having a difficult day, then the other can take over the responsibilities of the family, or, depending on the situation, both spouses can work as a team to finish the rest of the necessary tasks.

In today's world we run ourselves pretty ragged. There are a lot of responsibilities, activities, and outside commitments. When we are engaged in all these things, our patience, love, and kindness are usually the first things to go. In those moments, submitting ourselves to one another because of our faith can provide the extra boost necessary to muster a smile or gracious word. God knows how difficult it is to bite our tongues, to be loving after a difficult day at work and/or with the kids, and to put someone else's needs before our own. He wants to give us the tools and resources to enjoy our marriages, navigating the rocky moments with grace and mercy toward one another. He also knows we cannot do that relying on our own understanding and with our own skills and abilities. That is why He calls us to "submit to one another out of reverence for Christ." He lets us know that He sees what's going on and He is here to support and guide us.

The roles of husband and wife are unique in each relationship. Every couple has come together differently, and no two people are united in the same way, which is another reason God asks us to bring Him into our marriages. Only He knows the ins and outs of our stories, and only He can pinpoint the areas that need healing and love. Due to the unique nature of our relationships and personal journeys, I caution you from seeking counsel apart from God. It is difficult to process the intricacies of marriage. Having a safe place to confide in is life-giving. When we turn to well-meaning family or friends in our difficulties, they may cloud the situation, sometimes making it worse by projecting their personal experiences onto us. I am guilty of being an "Oh, me too" friend. When really, I have no idea. Unless we have walked through life in that person's shoes, we are only marginally familiar with the dynamics that are happening. Therefore, I encourage you to take your time, airing your grievances to God before venting to others.

You can bring your hurts to God. You can share your marriage with Him. He wants to walk alongside you, encourage you, and be a source of hope and strength. He will not ask you to be a doormat for your husband. He will not call you to be anything less than the woman He has designed you to be.

In case you have never been told before, I want to tell you something important now. You are allowed to scream at your Father. There is nothing wrong with screaming your hurt and wounds out to Him. Many nights I have been on my knees in gut-wrenching agony, furious with Him. Some devout Christians would argue with me, and I respect their opinion. I myself am respectful and proper by nature and prone to hold back my hurts and discomforts, shouldering them on my own. It takes a great deal for me to break. Therefore, when I am at a breaking point, I have a choice. Either I can continue carrying the burden on my own, which will only make me sick and hurt those around me, or I can choose to voice my emotional turmoil to my Father—the One who created me and ensures my existence, the One who has waited for me for centuries.

Our Abba wants to be invited into our conversation. If the only way for that to happen in the beginning is by turning to Him in the darkest moments, please do not hesitate. Over time the conversation will evolve.

Older couples holding hands

This is such a cliché, I know. It rings true for me at this stage in my life, however. When I see an older couple holding hands in a store or as they walk down a street, my heart melts because I know how rare an occurrence that is. A life can be taken too early; resentment can be rooted in the relationship, or a myriad of other things can prevent this closeness in a marriage after years of being together. An older couple holding hands is a living, breathing unicorn—a mythical sighting full of promise, hope, and joy. That is probably why they inspire me.

When I was a little girl, my great-grandma and I wrote letters to one another. Soon after my mom and (step)dad married, I was curious to hear about her life. She was born in the early 1900s, so she had lived in a very different era, and that fascinated me. Writing was difficult on her hands, so it took some time to receive her notes. She was also losing her memory, so she could not recall as many details as she would have liked.

One line from her correspondence inspired me to look beyond the pain of my biological father and the pieces of a family he had left. She wrote, "If couples today had half the love your great grandfather and I had, divorce lawyers would be out of business." Her words have been a rock for me to build my dreams upon.

Unfortunately, her soulmate was taken from her at an early age due to a drunk driver. She adored the man she married. Every day she would have his coffee ready for him, and it was a delight for her to care for him. Remember, this was a different era, when the women stayed home and the men went to work. Yet even though they held to very traditional roles, her husband saw a dream of hers and pushed her to go for it. After her kids were out of the house, she took to ceramics, and eventually, her husband built her a studio so she could teach classes at home and sell her own products.

Yes, she poured his coffee and made his supper. She folded his laundry and scrubbed his floors. And he appreciated her care of him. He saw a dream in her eye and made it happen for her. They inspire me. Their love was, perhaps, a little idealized by a young girl craving a beacon of hope and a direction for what marriage should look and feel like. It's a vision and truth I choose to hold onto no matter what.

When my great grandmother wrote the letter, her husband was gone; he had been buried several years earlier. Can you imagine a love like that? Every time I think about what I want for my marriage, I imagine the older couples who have been through war, childrearing, mortgages, and job changes yet still choose to be together. I know this is not always possible, but it is my inspiration for the tough days.

Come to the end of myself

As I shared earlier, becoming a wife was not the easiest transition for me. When Kurt and I look back, the long distance and lack of dating played a big part in our disruptive discovery process. However, I sometimes wonder: if we had dated and been in the same city, would the demons have still come with a vengeance? Was there a way to have prepared for my personal demons lying in wait? We attended marriage counseling and received a thumbs-up; therefore, I think the wounds were dormant, ready to rip open when my living situation changed.

I believe these details are really important to share with you. My husband and I did not have a lot of indicators warning us about the particular difficulties we would face as a married couple. We did not fight very often; we over-communicated, and we were fiercely committed to God and each other. One person suggested our constant conflict was due to the ages at which we married. (He was 33, and I was 27.) There might be some truth in that, but, in general, society shares a doubtful opinion about people who marry before the age of 25. Therefore, I caution drawing definitive conclusions without taking personalities and histories into consideration because each one of us is vulnerable to the attack of the wounds of our past and the all-consuming damage left in their wake.

Little did I know the early days of my marriage would be a picnic compared to what the future held. When deep wounds are left untended, they cry out for your attention and demand to be treated with love and care. Our journey with God is a constant discovery process. Whenever I believe life's turmoil is handled, opportunities arise for me to choose either to rely on Him or to soldier on and tackle the problem on my own.

My breaking point with God finally came a year and a half into my marriage. As I sat in the bathroom allowing the worst thoughts of the enemy to pour in my heart and mind, my six-month-old baby girl and husband were in the next room recovering from another soul-wrenching shouting match of accusations and misunderstandings. My parents were upstairs. Yes, my moment of absolute surrender was quite public. Our new family was visiting my parents in one of those tiny cabins in Tennessee during the Thanksgiving holiday.

You may already know where I'm going with this. A few years into our marriage, I discovered one of the triggers for my wounds to be reopened is a stressful family gathering. Bringing families together is not always joyful; it can be full of landmines and uncertainties. This bleeds into your marriage. But there is good news. Some of God's biggest breakthroughs happen in our most difficult moments because we are completely defenseless and cry out to Him. He is prevented from working in us before these catastrophic events because we do not invite Him; instead, we wait until the big shouting match has taken place, feelings have been hurt, and we are completely broken. You are not alone in your struggle. He has worked with me for decades, and I am finally starting to listen.

For this life-changing breakthrough, a lot of volatile pieces had to erupt at once. I quickly learned traveling ten hours with a new baby for a couple days is excruciatingly stressful, and at the time, I had no internal strength to say "no" and put up boundaries. This is an area I continue to struggle with because I am a recovering people pleaser. I want to fit in and make people happy. It's a deep craving rooted in my biological father's rejection.

As with any family gathering full of unspoken tension, adults battling their own wounds, and the added stress of caring for a six-month-old, we all walked away emotionally beaten up and bruised. Through the heartache, I struggled with a lie rooted in the baggage of my father's rejection, still unaware of how much it influenced my perception of reality. Because of the way I had spoken to my husband and how little he seemed to understand my struggles, I decided it was my responsibility to figure out how to care for our daughter without his involvement. I'm a Christian woman. I love my God and my husband, yet I wondered if my marriage would survive. It's hard to describe. On a very basic level of truth, like believing the sky is blue, I believed one of us would leave.

I've come to learn these are normal responses and thoughts for a child from a divorced home. While this may be common knowledge for other children of divorce, it wasn't for me. I never took the time to understand the baggage that comes with divorce. I did not expect to have these responses because I am fortunate enough to have a loving mother and (step)father. I had a front-row seat to a man with the best of intentions sweeping my mom off her feet and openly accepting my sister and me, becoming our dad. (I continue to witness mom and dad's loving relationship, which, at the time of the writing this book, has progressed through 22 years of marriage and is still going strong.) I truly believed the example of their marriage and the act of giving myself over to God at sixteen healed my previous hurts. Unfortunately, healing is not as simple as it is portrayed in a romantic comedy, even if you are one of the supporting actors.

It would be really nice to say the lie of the enemy concerning my marriage was erased from my mind and heart after doing x, y, and z. While today I can say this particular wound is completely submitted to God, it took years of fighting for my marriage to finally hand this insecurity and hurt over to my heavenly Father.

Our wounds will break open when they are left unattended, and when they do, our God will hold us and guide us through the mess. He is not surprised when we fight with our loved ones or make decisions that leave us broken and ashamed. We are not alone in these moments; nothing about us surprises Him.

Psalm 139 fascinates me. In it, we are told that God knows our every move and thought. At first, that kind of creeped me out. After all, some obvious questions come to mind: *Does He watch me sleep? Did He know I had that dirty thought?* Well, I am here to break it to you lovingly and gently—yes. Yes, He does. He knows all the crazy things we hide from everyone, even ourselves.

Why is this truth magical? Why is it a beautiful gift for those of us who are broken and full of wounds? And why are we so unwilling to face it? In moments of destruction and hurt, He knows. He is not surprised. He does not look on us with condemnation or disgust. He does not say, "Well, you know, I told you that's how this would go. If you had listened, this whole ordeal could have been avoided. You would be happy, and no one would be hurt." Ha. Like that's even possible! When we try to manage our own hurts, the only way to go is down on our knees and pray the destruction left in our wake is repairable. So, what does God say in those moments? How do you think He looks at *you*? What words does He wants to pour into *your* heart?

First, He opens His arms and invites you to come to Him. If that is too much, then He will sit with you and allow all your words to come out. He will say, "I love you. You are my child, and I see you are in pain." There is nothing more important to Him than being there with you in that moment. He is almighty and omnipresent; He can sit and care for you while performing miracles in hospitals and comforting families enduring difficult situations. In Scripture He says, "I will never leave you or forsake you" (Joshua 1:5 and Hebrews 13:5).

Usually we hide from God for two reasons. 1) We are ashamed of our actions. 2) We feel too small to be worth His time and effort. Who am I to ask God to be with me in this situation? Later in this book, you will discover exactly who you are to God, but for now, I will simply say, "You are a child of God."

Your Father wants to be with you in the dark moments of your marriage. He does not want you to navigate the complexities of marriage alone. In Scripture, we find invitation after invitation from Him seeking our attention and acceptance (Isaiah 55:1, Matthew 11:28-30, Luke 9:23-26, Luke 11:9-13, and more).

Will you accept His friend request?

You are not alone

When we are in the throes of brokenness, either allowing those around us to dominate us or living out the role of destroyer, it is difficult to believe there is a different path. During our darkest moments, we are unable to believe the truth that God loves us and wants to bring us out of the pain and suffering. These words can sound empty and full of false promises, but He truly can heal our personal wounds and show us how to guard ourselves from the demons lying in wait to rob us of our joy and worship.

If you become shy about sharing your wounds and hurts with the Lord, remember: He has seen it all. God has been a Father since the beginning of time, and His children have repeatedly chosen a path separate from Him. When His first children chose a shiny new object over Him, the Lord still clothed them and made a way for them to return (see Genesis 3). He is not surprised by your darkest moments, either. I invite you to give Him a chance.

My darkest moment, shared earlier in this chapter, came after my deepest wound was brought to my attention unexpectedly. A few weeks before the Thanksgiving trip, my husband and I had attended a spiritual retreat, which was the first step in discovering the root of my unexpected turmoil after saying, "I do." I remember handing my five-month-old over to a trusted friend who said, "Go. You need this." I didn't believe her; however, when God lines up all the pieces, it is never wise to walk away from the path He has prepared. My husband registered us for the retreat and encouraged me to go, and my dear friend had agreed to watch my newborn. So, we went.

During our time at the spiritual retreat, it became clear I was far from being the godly wife I was striving to be, and the root of this was to be found in what the retreat exercises help me label as my "death day"—the day that my biological father rejected me. Part of the retreat experience included identifying the worst experience of your early life in order to discover how it impacts your spiritual journey and your perception of God. When we did the exercise, I was not surprised that my father's rejection surfaced as my worst early experience. But until then, I had always treated my biological father's rejection as a piece of historical fact, not as a living part of who I am as a person.

As we went through different portions of the retreat, I slowly discovered there was a lot of baggage surrounding this one day in my past. In fact, the amount of baggage on my doorstep was taller than my head and unbearably heavy, blocking my view and my way forward. Instead of unpacking the crap and sorting through what to keep and get rid of, I allowed it to sit there and haunt me. It was constantly reminding me of my past, my shortcomings, and my "less thans."

A year and a half into my marriage, I had a lengthy list of "less thans" circling my mind. Because I yelled at my husband, I was "less than" an ideal wife. Because I was frustrated with my baby, I was "less than" a godly mother. Because I didn't work, I was "less than" a capable woman. Mind you, none of these were words people said to me; these were merely internal projections. Family and friends reading this book are probably shocked to learn the depths of my self-deprecation. But am I alone in this? What about you? Have you ever "less than'd" yourself?

While I looked at all the baggage, I realized I couldn't sort through it on my own, and I'd find bags wide open, laying on the front porch for everyone to see. My baggage was no longer a huge pile of boxes and suitcases. Now there were pieces of my heart and soul laying all over. Because I had chosen not to unpack those bags, take the time to see what was inside, and put the pieces in their place, the contents ended up littering my front lawn.

It was mortifying. I would be in the middle of a conversation with my husband and, all of a sudden, yell at him because he wasn't being kind or loving to me the way I expected him to. I would become infuriated over the laundry left on the floor. Why couldn't this man see that I had left my life to create a life with him and now I was a housekeeper? I was suddenly in a role I had never planned to sign up for, and those boxes and suitcases burst open.

When there's a mess in your soul, you get used to it after a while. The clutter becomes part of the landscape, and you don't realize the space it is taking up in your world.

How do we unpack this kind of baggage? After we finally realize that the cycle of insanity must be broken, a wise choice is to enter into conversation with God. I would like to say take it to a certain person, but at that time in my life, I had no one to talk to. Over time, I have realized God designed it that way on purpose. He wanted me to come only to Him because my questions were hard. If you do not currently have someone to go to and shed the weight of your soul, that might not be a bad thing. It could be a God thing.

This first step of my journey toward healing required some difficult self-evaluation, asking hard questions. The first thing I decided was that I did not want to be in this marriage. (Before you gasp, hold on tight!) I concluded the day-to-day realities of my marriage were not pleasing to God. I was not the wife He had called me to be, and both of us were miserable, which meant our daughter would be raised in a hostile home. These truths were unacceptable to me. After I concluded this marriage was not for me or Kurt, I immediately asked myself, *Do I want to be married to this man or someone else?*

Questions like this one are not just hard—they are excruciating. My answer came without hesitation. I knew I did not want to marry anyone else. I had waited a long time for this man to come into my life; the Lord had guided us to one another, and Kurt loved me as Christ did. So, I was in an interesting place. There was absolutely no one else I wanted to be married to, no temptation to leave and try something new, no appeal there. So, how can you not love the marriage you're in but not want to leave it? That's where God does some mighty, mighty things!

Even though I decided to stay, the next questions I asked myself were just as difficult. *How do I make this work? What do I need to change about myself to make a way for the marriage I envisioned on my wedding day?* Let me pause for a moment. Do you notice how those questions are worded? *How can **I** change?* One unsettling truth is that we have no ability to transform the people around us. The only change we can directly influence is the one within ourselves. It is tempting to point to others, saying, "Why aren't they doing this or that? I'm doing all this work, and they haven't taken any steps to change." We are human after all, and our nature is to compete and compare ourselves with each another. So many times, I have looked at my loving husband and thought, *I wish he would _____.* My encouragement to you, sweet sister, is to take hold of those thoughts and throw them into the garbage disposal. You are so much more than those thoughts. The Lord says our tongue "has the power of life and death" (Proverbs 18:21 NIV), and the words in our mind hold the same power.

As you take steps to look within, you will receive fruit from your hard work. Choosing to change the status quo of your relationship takes bravery because you are altering the dynamics of your situation. When you focus on bringing more grace and love into your marriage, you will be humbled and transformed. This is where the real work begins. You've decided to start looking at the baggage on your stoop to see what lies inside in order to free yourself (and your loved ones) from the demons stored there.

There are several practical approaches to begin this process since it can be very emotional and unsettling. You may not have a supportive community to walk alongside you during this self-discovery phase, and if that is the case, you must have a journal. I did not use a journal, but I could have avoided a lot of late nights if I had utilized this very basic and necessary tool for emotional cleansing. It was beyond my comprehension at that point in time to foresee the rollercoaster of growth, maturity, and healing God was taking me on.

The depth of my brokenness was unknown to me, which is not surprising since I still did not realize I was broken! God whispered there was more He wanted for me. He created me to be a loving, godly wife and to persevere in that calling. Therefore, it is with sisterly love I encourage you to grab a pen and some paper and write every day, even if all you write is, "Today was a day. My name is

_____. I am tired." By doing this, you are giving yourself the gift of a safe place to turn to at any time. You don't have to wait on someone to return your phone call or be in an understanding mood, and you don't need to take time to filter another's responses. A journal is an unbiased companion readily available to support you in your darkest moments. The trick is remembering to write at least one sentence every day so that you do not lose your momentum. You also need to find your rhythm and style. Each of us has a different way of processing emotions and thoughts. Find what works for you in your writing.

A warning for your journey: once you make the commitment to unpack your baggage, you will be tempted with distractions. When you seek to grow as a person, the enemy may tempt you to abandon that effort in favor of things like a worthwhile project, good deeds, serving your family, etc. Guard yourself against even these distractions for the first thirty days. Give yourself permission to write in a journal for ten minutes, seek counsel from a trusted source, and sit and cry as you mourn the loss of hopes and dreams you once held dear.

Healing from a father's rejection is no small matter. Our DNA comes from two people, and when one of them has left hurts, the wounds go to the core of who we are as a person. While this may sound dramatic or extreme, how can this not be the case?

If you are still skeptical or uncertain that the difficulties in your marriage are rooted in your father's rejection, take a moment and consider these questions to gauge where your frustration might be coming from in everyday moments:

1) When there is conflict in your family, how do you respond?
2) If your husband leaves dishes and laundry out, what are the thoughts running through your mind?
3) When was the last time you shared your dreams with your spouse?

You may be wondering what laundry has to do with your father.

Well, when I looked at the real reasons I would become frustrated with my husband for leaving his socks out, I found two: 1) I think he's being lazy, and 2) I believe his action shows that he disrespects me. As I began to unpack my baggage, I realized that if my primary thought was that he was being lazy, then I would become frustrated and grumble a little, but when I noticed this train of thought, I could call it out. Then, I would pray for the opportunity to care for my husband.

This awareness and proactive behavior helped me to go tell him in a normal tone of voice that I would appreciate him using the laundry basket. My words and actions would come from a loving place, even if I still felt frustrated. However, if my primary thought was that he was disrespecting me, I would find myself beginning to question why I was staying home to care for our family and if it was worth my time and talents. Then I would wonder what it would be like not to be forced to do laundry regularly and care for people who do not seem to appreciate my skills. If I allowed this train of thought to go on any longer, which it always did, I would start to see all the ways my husband "disrespected" me. Throughout a typical day, my thoughts would spiral along these lines:

"Here I am changing the diaper while he sits there on the couch."
"Yep. It's just ME washing the dishes and cleaning up after dinner."

Then, my thoughts would digress into wondering what he's worth, why I even bother serving him, and ways life could be better.

Now, I'm not saying these thoughts will ever go away completely. We are human and work hard to care for the lives we are given. There will be frustrating days, excruciatingly human moments, and words said in moments of anger. It is the combination and buildup of these thoughts that is so damaging, though. For me they always led to darker thoughts, such as, *He doesn't really want to be married. He just likes the convenience.* That was what my biological father wanted—the convenience of a wife but not the complications of a family.

I married a 33-year-old bachelor, and I really had no idea the first year of marriage would be a difficult transition for him. (Ok, you can stop laughing now.) While his responses were often simply due to this huge life change, I often interpreted them as the precursors of total rejection. You see, when we are wounded, seeds of doubt and uncertainty are planted. Then, common frustrations lead to negative thoughts that, if left unchecked, nurture those seeds of doubt, and the fruit they bear is the destruction and death of relationship.

Journal Prompt

Marriage is an incredibly deep topic to cover, and each one of our marriages looks different. I appreciate you taking the time to walk through my darkest moments with me. My hope is that by sharing my hardest stories, so far, that it will help you release any guilt or shame surrounding yours so that you feel free to reach out for support and love.

When we have very human moments, a natural response is to clam up and hide our difficulties from the world. We live in a "highlight-reel" world where most people are not vulnerable with the reality of their lives. While blasting our struggles on social media is not a healthy response, reaching out to our dearest friends during times of turmoil should always be encouraged. I hope you feel released to turn to a trusted, safe place and discover love and grace.

1) I married my husband because _____.

2) My husband makes me smile when _____.

3) Is your marriage in a healthy place? Explain.

4) Do you dream with your spouse? If so, what are you both dreaming about? If not, what would you like to start dreaming about with him?

5) Do you invite God into your marriage? How could you invite God into the day to day dynamics more often?

Prayer

Dear Lord, thank you for my sisters in Christ who walk the journey of married life alongside me. I am so thankful for them and the spirit they bring to their families. You delight in our relationships and the covenant we have made before You. Please continue to bring women into my life who worship You and center their worlds on You so that we may encourage each other and build each other up in times of difficulty. Thank you for my husband, one of Your sons. I pray you show me the unique shape of his character, the different ways You delight in him, and how I can love him as You designed. I confess it may be difficult for me to invite You, Father, into my darkest places, and I ask You to continue to walk alongside me and show me Your grace and love. I yearn to honor You in my marriage. Amen.

4

Motherhood

Have mercy on me, Lord, for I am faint;
heal me, Lord, for my bones are in agony.
My soul is in deep anguish. How long, Lord, how long?
– Psalm 6:2-3 (NIV)

As I stared at my small humans, brought into my world through the grace of God, the thought of leaving and never returning crossed my mind. What would life look like for them without me here? These thoughts were not rooted in the belief they'd be better off without me; no, those thoughts had crossed my mind in the past but were rooted in a different struggle. The source for considering a new reality came from a selfish emotion. I thought my children were acting out because they disrespected me. My one-, two-, and four-year-olds were testing boundaries, screaming throughout the day, and navigating the world the way they wanted, and I was beginning to believe it was due to a conscious desire to disobey me. They knew not to jump on the couch or paint on the walls, but instead of honoring their mother, they chose to act out in disobedience, *demonstrating that they did not love me.* Yes, at some point during the long days and short weeks, I began to believe my children's actions reflected their feelings toward me as their mother. How could they not like the woman who chose to stay home to care for them, feed them, clothe them, and provide them with opportunities for joy?

The darkness did not stop there. I continued to struggle with an unfamiliar rage living inside of me. Prior to this dark period, I faced the realities of PTSD, postpartum depression, military-spouse depression, and grief over the loss of a community. Becoming a mom was not the only life-altering transition in my life, but it has proven to be the most difficult to understand. I hear that is normal, thankfully. As I tried to wrap my head around the storm inside, I sat in my favorite room of our home, flooded with emotion and insecurity. I wondered if my little ones wanted me as their mama. After all, if they loved and respected me, then their actions would reflect those feelings (and validate my place in their world). This lie filtered into my mind and heart and took root without my notice.

Completely broken, I sat in our beautiful home as the thought of leaving flooded my mind, quickly followed by shame and guilt consuming my heart and soul. These little ones didn't know any better—why would they want the person who makes their food and tucks them in at night to leave?

This is one of those dark places of motherhood I believe we are scared to talk about. We don't discuss our most vulnerable human moments and the soul-cutting struggles we encounter in the journey of raising small humans because we fear shame, discomfort, and judgment. The reasons I am writing this book and sharing my story with you are to break the silence, provide a safe place for you, and share the hope for change. More women walk around in shame and fear than we are aware of because discussion about these struggles is not encouraged. Granted, these aren't topics to bring up at dinner parties; however, hiding behind closed doors and enveloping ourselves in shame and guilt is not the way we were intended to live out our days on this planet. I believe we underestimate the power of a ray of pure light cutting into darkness—one ray can change the trajectory of a life. I know this because that is what happened for me.

I was battling an unknown demon and eventually opened up about my struggle. I am blessed to have relationships with three people who each shined a ray of light into my world while I continued to hide my pain from everyone else. In their love and grace, I found my first steps of healing. They did not judge me, nor did they placate me with empty words. My moments with them were filled with love, compassion, and encouragement. Their words and mercy were an extension of our Father's unconditional love, and I soaked it up.

There is a little more to tell you about the day I sat in my favorite seat and broke. No doubt, I was in a dark place. Have you ever been in a dark place and weren't quite sure how you got there? You look around, and the landscape is not as you remember. The environment has changed, and the people are unrecognizable, especially the one in the mirror. In my darkest season, my view of motherhood seemed to shift in an instant. No longer was the loving, caring, patient mama sitting on the floor with her children. A raging monster had taken over her body and was doing her best to reenact Godzilla's takeover of New York City.

If you already have a relationship Christ, you might be able to recognize the flesh and the enemy working in those moments and the thoughts struggling to take hold of your mind. The part that really surprised me is that I could not stop them! I know God, and I usually feel in sync with Him (at least as much as I know how to be at this point in my journey), and I could not shut out the enemy. My weary soul was consumed with brokenness. And I crossed a line.

I share the line I crossed to hopefully release you from the lines you may have crossed and to show you there is no perfection in our flesh. However, thankfully, there is redemption in God, and you can choose another path. No matter what you have done or said, your past does not have to define your future. Will you allow me to show you a different choice? Are you open to love? Are you willing to allow healing?

Ok, with those seeds planted, let's get back to the end of my rope… On second thought, let's wait a moment. Isn't it insane how God will allow us to walk through life and discover what the world is about? We are so stubborn and human that it usually takes coming to the end of ourselves for us to FINALLY get out of our own way and allow God to work in us. Allowing Him to work in us is not like getting a manicure; it's not just about smoothing a few rough edges and putting on some polish—there is a lot of junk to be evaluated and removed! It's like going into a hoarder's house and making a clean sweep. Have you seen one of those hoarder shows? There are insects and rodents hiding in places no one would expect, and the pain and hurt at the root of the hoarding is complex. Not only are you cleaning the house, but you are also opening up the heart and soul of the homeowner.

When I finally arrived at the end of my rope—the scary, dark place—change did not happen overnight. I lived in that very dark place for a couple months believing it was temporary or due to lack of sleep. And, yes, sometimes there are dietary and health factors impacting our behavior, but after those are addressed and we are still not fully ourselves, then it is time to look inside and uncover the layers. However, instead of seeking help or relying on anyone, I continued to forge ahead, and I broke.

As I continued to listen to the enemy and believe my children's actions reflected their lack of love for me, I looked at them and asked, "Do you want me as your mama?" Some of you may be horrified by this question, and I'm so thankful you are. Even if you haven't asked such a question, you may still understand the brokenness of feeling undervalued, invisible, and worthless.

Right away, I knew I had crossed a line, and as I asked the question and continued to think about it for days afterwards, I told God, "Oh, this is what my father felt like. Every time I did not follow his rules exactly, this is how he felt."

I was horrified. My children had done nothing out of the ordinary. I have a master's degree in early childhood education, so I am fully aware that my children were acting their age and that absolutely none of their actions reflected a lack of love for me.

I was blindsided by rejection from the past, and it was leaking all over my family.

When I realized my emotions mirrored the ones I felt when my biological father rejected me, one memory came to mind…

One day when I was trying to help my daddy clean up the kitchen, I put watermelon seeds down the drain. I was disciplined with a punishment that bruised my skin and hurtful words that bruised my heart. I knew exactly what my children were feeling because I was old enough to remember that situation yet still young enough to adore my daddy.

Now, to my absolute shame, I found myself in his shoes. I'm not quite sure how I feel about viewing the world from his perspective. It's an extremely selfish vantage point, and living a life from a selfish perspective has consequences for decades. In fact, the damage can be felt for *generations*. And that's the suitcase I'd like to unpack in this chapter: generational sin.

If you had asked me before that day in my kitchen if my father's abandonment had affected my parenting, I would have looked at you cross-eyed and confidently denied it. My mom and (step)dad were the central figures of my teenage years and the ones I look to for guidance, so why would I be influenced by someone who wasn't really part of the picture? I discovered it's not that simple.

We are a product of our environments, whether we choose to recall those memories or not. Our childhood is imprinted on our core, and we carry those impressions, thoughts, ideas, and experiences into adulthood. Some pieces will lie dormant; others we happily use as a guide to decision-making, and some will pop into our reality rather suddenly. This was not a truth I had ever considered. My education taught me that we carry with us the relationships we see unfolding in our preschool years. I remember saying to my husband, "I don't want our children to grow up with this person as their mother. This is not who I am. Brasher is only a year old, but this is who he is being conditioned to identify as his mom. I don't like it."

Even though I knew my behaviors were being impressed upon my son, becoming the only way he knew me, and my girls were starting to acclimate to this new version of me, it took coming to the end of my rope for me to see the correlation of my childhood environment with my parenting style. When I was stopped in my tracks and made to look in the mirror, it all became clear. You may still be in turmoil, too, unsure what is throwing your world off. Let's take a moment and discover if you are battling generational sin.

I have a question I'd like to ask, and it may make you a little uncomfortable. However, I stress to you the importance of thinking on this question and opening yourself up to seeking the answer. Is there a piece of your parenting that reflects the rejection of your father? It could be a subtle way of talking with your children, expectations you have for them, or a self-protective guarding of your heart. We are a product of our parents, whether we like it or not. When we face this truth and acknowledge it, we can then take daily actions to tweak or eliminate behaviors we refuse to carry on and share with our children. We can "rewrite the script." We do not have to pass down the same legacy given to us.

Maybe you received a pretty great legacy and just want to make a few tweaks here and there, or maybe you are in a dark place feeling desperate to change the mood of your home and transform yourself into the mom you long to be. Wherever you are today, there is no reason you cannot become the mom you desire to be. One step every day with God can lead to a new legacy for your family. You can change what habits are given to your children and possibly even the words that will come out of their mouths to your grandbabies.

If your children are grown, you can still enable your family to rewrite their scripts and break generational sins. How? By allowing them to live their journey and by relying on your Father to guide you during difficult moments. My mother does not do it perfectly, but she does it with a fierceness. She constantly encourages me to rewrite my story and embrace the life I desire for my children. It's not easy for her; sometimes there is conflict and feelings are hurt. I love her for being courageous and encouraging. I am a recovering people pleaser and would not be writing this story without her blessing. So, even as the mother of grown children, you have the opportunity to rewrite the legacy: how will you channel the gift of influence?

As we confront the reality of generational sin and begin looking in the mirror, the reflection can be unsettling. It can be scary to stop and look inside. When we believe everyone else has it mostly together and is doing life right, then we can easily choose to ignore our issues by focusing on (and becoming distracted by) the busyness of life. We can say to ourselves, *If I do "this," then I'm a good mom. If I try "that," then my kiddos will grow up well-rounded and with great opportunities.* Instead of allowing ourselves the space to reflect on the inner workings of our home, we try to patch up the turmoil or fix it with outside solutions. But outside solutions will never work if the true source of hostility, miscommunication, and lack of connection is lying within ourselves. If we are brave enough to take some time and pause, look within, and come to a safe place to digest the pain, our families' stories can be rewritten. With God's help, *we can* repair damaged relationships, pour love into our marriages and children, and find ways to be accepting and understanding.

When there is hurt and pain within us, it is nearly impossible to pour out love and compassion because we have little capacity to sit, listen, and receive the pain and hurt of our loved ones. Instead, we turn it back on them, process their voices in unhealthy ways, and then tear ourselves down because we should be better than this.

Wow. This is an intense topic, right? Raising babies is a beautiful gift with great responsibility, and one I take to heart. Fortunately, there is so much light to be had in this journey, and no reason we cannot be the moms we long to be. I share the truth of generational sin in motherhood because it is not a topic I see covered often and it started to rob me of my identity and eliminate the joy I could have in being part of my children's journeys from birth.

If you are a mama, you have most likely walked the trenches of diapers, potty-training, and first steps. You may even have gotten as far into the journey as navigating driver's licenses and weddings. But no matter how far you are into motherhood, an earthly father's rejection can show up when you least expect it. I desire to arm you for battle so that when the enemy comes knocking, you can fight back and bring God's blazing light of truth into those moments. You are worthy and beautiful and deserving of light to shine through you and into your home.

Generational sin's place in our home

Generational sin is a big concept. What does this even mean? Is it a Christianese concept created only to make us feel worse about ourselves or to shift the blame for our actions? Have we developed a new way to process the way we were raised and then not take responsibility for who we are as adults? Generational sin is rooted in the habits of our ancestors. As families we are linked to previous generations through finances, beliefs, values, and professions; for better and for worse.

In biblical times children were held responsible for their parents' actions and could go into slavery if they were unable to pay taxes or tithe to the king. The use of indentured servants continued into the twentieth century when families paid for their father's debts. In the present time, there are some cultures where the honor of a family is critical in social standing, and if someone breaks societal rules, then their family falls from grace for generations.

In addressing generational sin, God's Word reflects a scientific fact: as children we are influenced by our environment. By the age of four, we are already programmed to respond to the world around us. The way we see adults interact is our reference point for how we will navigate relationships in our world as we mature, and we will act out these tendencies with very little conscious thought about them. So, you might begin looking for generational sin in one of those suitcases lying on your doorstep if you have had children out of wedlock, if you yell as a regular form of communication, if you lie to save face, if you use negative self-talk, or if you can label any number of other unhealthy strategies for coping with fear, relationships, or life.

Not many would view negative self-talk as a sin; however, the Lord tells us our tongues either bring life or death. If we are speaking negatively about ourselves, what prevents us from speaking ill of those around us, even our children? Are we to speak life or death over the image of God? After all, we are made in His image.

A mother's actions

I heard a woman describe her mother in a beautiful way that has helped me as I try to parent through Christ and has given me hope for the legacy I will leave my children. As she spoke lovingly of her mother, this woman painted a picture of her mom sitting at the kitchen table in the mornings and spending time with her Father. She would sit with her book open, a journal by her side, and often a pen in hand. This is who I want to be. The woman went on to say that the greatest gift her mother gave her was a glimpse at what it looks like to be a daughter of Christ. Her mother went to the Lord every day and spent time with Him. She honored Him with her first hours, and her daughters saw their mom as more than a homemaker. They saw her as a child delighting in her Father's presence.

This is the vision I want to leave for my children—a vision of their mother navigating the ups and downs of life at the feet of the Father and being with Him. I was humbled and delighted in this vision. There was someone waiting for me every morning to share in the journey of motherhood. Not only did I have my husband, but I also had my Father. As I reflected on the beauty of sitting with Him every day, I realized I did not have to navigate the complexities of childrearing alone. He would be there to pick me up, hold me close, and speak truth into me.

One of the reasons I fell in love with this vision is that it appeared possible. I could sit at my table, open a book, and spend time with the Lord. The idea of striving to be the kind of mom who is always ready to embrace her child after a fight, is available for artwork at the drop of a hat, reads stories for hours and never gets bored seems exhausting. In fact, those moms have always intimidated me. During my dark days, I was afraid to utter a word due to the damage I might cause to the little souls in my care. I was fearful of hurting them in ways that were irreparable. But sitting? Reading? Just being present before God? I could do that. This seemed manageable. Maybe, just maybe, I wouldn't be horrible at this.

Even though I love this vision, I am still navigating how to make it a consistent reality. My kids are still young; mornings are hectic, and life can feel like a hot mess. However, I still hang on to this vision of spending time with God daily and having Him with me along the journey. This vision is life-giving, and I still hope to take a step toward this legacy every day. The vision of the mom sitting at the table with her journal and Bible reminds me that I do not have to do this alone.

We are invited to sit with the Lord every day and share our deepest hurts and greatest desires. He knows them already. He's waiting for us to invite Him to share our journey.

Sins of the father

When I finally realized the root of my anguish, I turned to our true Father. While I didn't know the exact Scripture, I knew God had sent His Son to die for our sins so we do not have to carry on the sins of our earthly fathers. I clung to this truth and poured out my heart to Abba. It never occurred to me that my biological father's approach to parenting would affect my parenting style. I knew I would do more than send a child support check and ask about my children's weight and safe sex habits. And because I am naturally wired to be more involved than my biological father is, I never gave a thought to his influence on my parenting.

Whether you are first hearing about generational sin in this book or you were already aware of its existence, I would like to assure you of the truth that God frees us. In Jeremiah 31:29-34, we are told, "When that time comes [referencing Christ's coming to Earth], people will no longer say, 'The parents have eaten sour grapes, but the children's teeth have grown numb.' Rather, each person will die for his own sins. The teeth of the person who eats the sour grapes will themselves grow numb. 'Indeed, a time is coming,' says the Lord, 'when I will make a new covenant with the people of Israel and Judah.'"

For centuries the sins of the father were passed on to the children. Our very being is wired to take on the sins of the previous generation; we are not exempt from feeling the weight of their mistakes and choices. However, one of the gifts God gave us when He sent His Son to die for us was to free us from having to bear the weight of our fathers' sins. We do not have to carry with us the burdens of their choices when we have a relationship with Christ.

If we don't have a relationship with Christ, then we can respond to the sins of our fathers in two ways. The first is a continuance of those sins because of our unawareness of them. We can pass them on to the next generation through our words and actions. The other response is to overcompensate. For example, my mom always pushed me to be a better person than she is. She provided a foundation and expected me to build upon it for future generations. My generation has taken this to an extreme. We try to give our children so much more than we had and insulate them from negative consequences. This extreme is unsettling because if we hand everything to our children, how in the world will they learn to function for themselves and lead their children and grandchildren? We are so scared of repeating what our parents did that we are overcompensating.

So, how do we overcome generational sin through Christ?

Generational sin

If you are currently mothering small children, I just want to send you a hug right now...and a big box of chocolates and a case of coffee—the stimulants necessary to navigate the "trench years." Whether you have showered today or last week, you look stunning. Seriously. You're awake, breathing, and reading a book! At this point you are a fully-functioning adult and a contributing member of society. Well done.

This next part is going to be a little tricky, and I ask you to stick with me through it. If you need to throw the book across the room, please do. Then come pick it up, perhaps pour yourself a glass wine, and continue. The reason I believe this next part may be a little difficult is that we are going to discuss generational sin in more detail. I really wish someone had forewarned me about this beautiful piece of parenthood *(please hear my socially-appropriate sarcasm there)*.

The extreme exhaustion of becoming a mother took me by surprise. The lack of wanting to be intimate with my husband—ever again—was a real shock. And my body. Let's not even go there. I'm still trying to figure out what she is all about. Yes, I've decided there is me, and then there is my body. One day we will be one again, and she won't look like such a stranger.

On top of all that, my identity was hijacked and thrown out the window! Suddenly, I was not Trish anymore. I was Ellewyn's mom, and then…then… I found myself saying all the words my mother used to say. Ugh. Seriously? Not only had I lost all the good things in life (sleeping, sex, and an identity), but I had also become my mother. As I have always done with most things in life, I pulled up my big girl panties and logically processed this new reality—begrudgingly, of course. However, I did adjust.

My thought process went something like this: Alright. Fine. I'll adjust. My mom really isn't that bad, and after some sleep, I can learn to tweak her sayings and then embrace the ones my filter cannot stop. Sleep? Ok, I'll adopt the phrase, "Eh. No big deal. I'll sleep when I'm dead." I can power through this. After all, I did shiftwork for five years. My body and brain will adjust; it's not the end of the world. Oh? No more Trish? Just Ellewyn's mom? Again, ok. This identity helps me connect with some pretty cool gals I otherwise wouldn't have met. I might be able to dig this, and that Ellewyn girl is pretty fantastic.

It took a few years, but I was pretty sure I made the adjustment. I was feeling better about my role as mom with three little ones and a husband in the Army. I could do this. *We* could do this.

Then, it happened. Demons previously believed to be healed reared their ugly heads. Thoughts that were foreign to me spun around in my mind, and words that were unlike me came pouring out of my mouth as I struggled to deal with a willful two-year-old and smart-mouthed four-year-old. The woman in the mirror no longer looked like me because I was angry, bone-deep angry. This woman I no longer knew was saying things that didn't make sense. Insecurities come forth that cripple my very foundation and were laid bare for the entire family to see. Deep-rooted shame descended into my very being.

Generational sin had arrived on my doorstep, and it was ready to be unpacked. Where was the notice? I did not receive a shipping notification in my email inbox. Why was it here? Who dropped it off? Ugh. What did this even mean? I didn't know where to start.

Maybe you aren't sure what generational sin is, which is quite common because it's quite a big topic to unpack. The simple version is: the behaviors and perspectives of our parents and/or grandparents that come flooding into our present relationships. Adopting the behaviors and mindsets we saw as children is a natural part of growing up and transitioning into adulthood. There is no way to avoid this; it's scientific. But knowing what generational sin is doesn't really relieve the stress or worry about reliving the sins of our fathers, does it? I feel the same way.

I was wrecked when the sins of my biological father came brutally knocking on the door of my home. This suitcase was opened up when it landed on my front porch because, like I said before, I did not receive a delivery notification and was unaware of the baggage. The first thing I did when I realized I was treating my children as my biological father had treated me was to weep in absolute mortification. How could this be happening? Who was this person I had turned into? And not only was I emulating him, but I was also bringing the most painful parts of my mom into our home, too. Oh, the heartache! My older girls knew mommy wasn't this person and weren't scared of me yet, even though they were getting there, but my little boy had only existed for nine months. He was starting to experience equal parts of his true mom and the beast that had taken up residence in her place.

If you are in a similar situation, if you have ever acted in a way not true to your character, then you know the shame and guilt waiting to engulf you when the out-of-body experience is over. For a while I blamed my actions on the kids' developmental changes and my lack of sleep. Other times I would revert to complete denial about the chaos taking over our home.

Mama, I want to share with you some beautiful truths. You do not have to stay in this place, and no one expects you to navigate it alone. If you are too ashamed to share with a friend or two, then know there is One you can always share with, and He won't be surprised by what is going on. God is waiting for you to invite Him into the mess.

You do not have to be currently living in this stage to invite Him into your pain, though. We all have days we wish we could rewrite and moments we never wish to repeat. Whether your kids are grown or still in diapers, God is ready to sit with you and heal the hurt.

I am not free of these attacks, sweet mama. While I don't live in fear of the day and worry how I will act if one happens, there is a constant need to be vigilant during these days of littles. One of my saving graces has been inviting people into the mess. There are two women I meet with regularly, and we share our walk together with no judgments or expectations. I was mortified to share with them what was happening because they are both kind, gentle, fierce women of God; however, the stirring of the Spirit was within me. In addition, we had met for over two years, and I'd known them longer. When I shared, there was so much love and compassion in their eyes—no judgment. Sweet mama, there is no judgment today for you either, only arms full of compassion.

After I shared my battle with these women, I posted a Facebook request asking for godly mama resources that I didn't have to read. I was too busy running after three little kiddos, building a business, and honoring my marriage to read a book. My friends rallied around me, even though I did not pour out all my struggles online. They surrounded me and shared several resources. The ones that have made the most difference are the "God-Centered Mom" and "Risen Motherhood" podcasts. There are also incredible books, conferences, and Bible studies available for comfort and encouragement.

At my lowest point, I needed to hear uplifting words and receive encouragement and grace. The first podcast I listened to was about grace and the way the Lord wants us to raise up our children. My world shifted because now I could spend time every day with women who desired the same thing I did. They struggled with human moments and still loved their families. I invited truth and goodness into my home, and when I laid my weakness at the altar and accepted the fact that I could not fix myself on my own, a paradigm shifted. I was no longer a lone wolf from 7am-5:30pm, raising children and fighting for sanity. I was a woman armed with the love of my Father and an army of God-fearing mamas ready to fight the battle with me. No longer did I call my husband to desperately apologize for being a failed wife and mother. My armor was ready to be put on at a moment's notice. You can do this, too.

By the grace of God, we do not have to live in the sin of our fathers.

Journal Prompt

Oh, my sweet mama, we are on a battlefield, and I want to arm us with words of strength and redemption.

1) Name one person/resource that brings you life. How is your cup filled?

2) What is one thing about your mothering style that you love? How do you connect with your children this way?

3) Finish this sentence: One of my strengths as a mom is _____. (You have at least one—do NOT leave this blank!!)

Prayer

Dear Lord, thank You for the beautiful blessing of being a mother. I am humbled by the gift of raising one of Your children. I am also frustrated, overwhelmed, and consumed by the responsibility and complexity of motherhood. Please be with me on this battlefield, and never leave my side. Please do not abandon me in the trenches when I lose sight of Your glory and promises. I ask for You to bring women alongside me who will show me grace and impart wisdom so that I can do more than survive. My prayer is to honor You through the raising of my children, and I know this cannot be done on my own. Please heal my hurts, guilts, and shoulda-wouldas. Thank You for loving me and never abandoning me. Amen.

5

Self – Reliance

"Blessed is the man who trusts in the Lord, whose trust is the Lord. He is like a tree planted by water, that sends out its roots by the stream, and does not fear when heat comes, for its leaves remain green, and is not anxious in the year of drought, for it does not cease to bear fruit." - Jeremiah 17:7-8

Once there was a young man who was abandoned by his family and left for dead. He ended up in a close relationship God because he was able to see the difference between God and family and allow himself to trust after being rejected and turned away. Eventually, God led him to a place of service and honor. Instead of choosing to shut out all sources of love and compassion, he leaned on the one family member he could trust—his heavenly Father. This young man was Joseph, and we can read his story in the Bible in Genesis.

Joseph was the youngest in a family of twelve boys, and, as with most babies, he was the favorite. His parents doted on him and treasured him above his brothers. Like any family, the other brothers were not thrilled by the fact that their youngest brother, who had not worked as hard as they had or shouldered the same responsibilities, was favored. Shouldn't they be held in higher regard? Their actions were worthy of acknowledgement and praise. What had the youngest done? Nothing. The brothers took matters into their own hands, sold Joseph into slavery, and told their father Joseph had been killed. They believed they had eliminated a distraction that was limiting their parents' love and adoration for them.

Joseph was not an ignorant young man; he knew why his brothers had sold him into slavery. They were jealous of him and hated his very existence. While Joseph was not rejected by his father, he was abandoned by his family and sold into slavery. Still, during each situation he encountered, the Lord was with him. The Lord protected him during his first assignment as a slave, working in a master's home in a position almost equal to the master himself. Joseph even said, "With me in charge my master does not concern himself with anything in the house; everything he owns he has entrusted to my care. No one is greater in this house than I am" (Genesis 39:8-9, NIV). This position would not last, however.

Joseph was pursued by his master's wife, and when he refused to sleep with her, she lied about him to her husband, saying Joseph had come after her. Joseph could have been put to death; instead, he was sent to prison, where the Lord still watched over him.

Joseph's family and his master's wife acted out of selfishness. The master, who had trusted Joseph with everything, turned on him because of his wife's accusations. A second time in his life, Joseph was abandoned by those he trusted, and he had a choice. Either he could lose all hope and believe the lies the world continued to tell him, or he could turn to God and choose His truth. We are in the same boat as Joseph when the people around us say we are unworthy, not enough, or less than. We have a choice, too. We can either believe them and wear the lies of the world or choose to fight for the truth.

No matter what happens in our lives, God is always with us. It may not look like it in the moment because relationships are full of turmoil; our emotions are all over the place, and our life circumstances are less than we would prefer. But our circumstances do not always reflect truth, especially when we have allowed the lies of the world to take root in us. When these lies are living inside our hearts, they pour out of us and become the reality we live in. Joseph could not have been feeling loved and protected when he was given over to a slavery caravan headed for Egypt or when his master's wife turned against him and he was thrown into prison. However, during those trials, God was still with Joseph.

Your journey

We are often tempted to rely on our own understanding and expectations when bad things happen to us. When our earthly father abandons us or repeatedly speaks unkind words to us, it is tempting to believe all adults are evil and the world is against us. We can put up walls and choose to tackle mountains on our own. It becomes difficult for others to penetrate our defenses, and we hesitate to let anyone in. Let's be honest, when we are in self-reliant mode, we don't allow an opportunity to come for someone to let us down, betray us, or hurt us.

Not only is our natural inclination to push people away and try to navigate the world on our own, but society also sends messages to affirm that this is the best way forward. Our culture encourages the aloof, strong, self-reliant approach. And if we were let down repeatedly in the past, we find it safer to shut out the loved ones in our lives and the mentors ready to assist us.

Being part of a family is tough stuff. (This is true for both the family you are born into and the one you choose.) Whether you have a small, distant family or a very involved, blended one, you will have complications as you interact in those relationships. So, when things go horribly wrong—which they will—how should you respond? How can you prevent yourself from reverting to old behaviors you are trying to move past? Whether your tendency is to get angry and lash out, drop off the face of the earth and ghost on the family, or turn passive aggressive and manipulative, there is a better way. I have tried all those responses, and none has left me feeling peaceful, whole, and certain of myself.

In the worst situations, even in the face of guaranteed conflict at social gatherings, there is an approach that has brought me peace and understanding. That approach is to remember that God is with me and to ask Him for assistance. I say something like, "Ok, God, this person is driving me crazy, but I don't want to cause a scene or upset anyone. Can You please bring me peace? Help me out? Something? Thank You!" My words don't have to be eloquent or fancy; in fact, when I'm in an emotional state, my words come out very simply. I've found life to be more fulfilling if I'm blunt with God and not my loved ones during difficult moments.

Another way to navigate the ups and downs of relationships is to have a couple of people who are always on your side. I believe God's love is reflected through those people who listen on a bad day, tell you the hard truth (with love), and are able to make you laugh. When work or life becomes difficult, it is easy to start shutting people out. It took a decade or two for me to discover that this was my habit, part of it deeply rooted in my father's rejection. If he didn't love me at my cutest and sweetest times of life, how could someone else accept my crazy-hot mess exploding right now?

I have encouraging words, friend. No matter what is happening in your world, God has placed people in your life to show you the love He wants you to know. Accept them. Make room for them. Through those relationships you're going to discover God's presence in humanity. It's scary. I get it. You've already been rejected in one of the worst ways. Now I'm saying, "Put yourself out there again. Come on. Sure, someone else might say you're not good enough, but you might find someone who extends God's love to you when you need it most." Choosing to be part of community is a daily choice (and sometimes a minute-by-minute choice).

I've lived both ways—on my own with the world shut out and in the midst of godly community, where I allowed people to be part of my journey and speak into my life. I won't say choosing community is all sunshine and roses, but here's the thing… You'll never see the sunshine or smell the roses when you are on an isolated journey. The landscape is harsh, cold, and full of jagged drop-offs when we are guarded and armed to fight each person who comes along and may challenge our thoughts and ideas. And when we are waiting for rejection and anticipating disappointment, the world will always deliver.

The only way to experience something different is to try a new approach to your everyday routine. You know that saying, "Why do you expect different results when you continue to do the same thing?" When you keep your guard up and don't allow others to sit with you awhile, then you will continue to reap the same results. Is that what you want? Do you want the rest of your days on this earth to be what they have been? I believe you picked this book up for a reason. Let's take the opportunity to dream a little. You're in a safe place. It's just you, the pages of this book, and God (yep, He's here with you, too). So, let's take the first step and dream a little. Think about it. What would an ideal evening look like? Or a weekend?

Maybe even a holiday? If you haven't dreamed in a while, this may take some time to sort through.

The reason I encourage you to dream again and open yourself up to what could be is that it will enable you to write your own future. In my personal journey, I left the baggage untended, which led to unexpected surprises when I married and became a mother of three. Instead of turning to God and seeking His love, I felt shame and guilt for being broken. I believed there was something wrong with me for not having my act together as a wife and mother.

I'll be completely honest, I'm a little nervous to see what the rest of my life has in store. There may be more unexpected baggage delivered at the drop of a hat. However, my steps forward are assured because I have finally, after much fighting and deliberation, acknowledged God as my loving Father and accepted His unconditional love as truth.

My compass

As I reflect on the past and remember the times my baggage came busting open, I can see that there was one person who would remind me I was loved. When you've been abandoned and rejected, it can be difficult to believe anyone sees your worth. It is easier to believe these lies of the world: "Be strong. Rely on yourself. You're the only one you can depend on." So, what do we do with our rejection? How do we move forward in a functional way that doesn't leave pure devastation in our wake?

We pause. We think. We remember. There is almost always at least one person in our past who showed us love. This person may have been a member of a host family, a police officer, a grandparent, or a teacher. He or she may only have been able to show us love and support for a short time rather than through an ongoing relationship. The memory of this person may be a distant one. Even so, *someone* was once there for us.

My person was my mom. Growing up, I had the wonderful blessing of the fierce love of a mom. She chose to battle the world and make a new way for my sister and me when the damage was becoming too great. I was blessed even more when the man she married later turned out to be my dad, my heart father. I've always known how lucky I am. There are countless young ladies who are not given an earthly father who loves and cares for them. I know the

Lord was watching over me with my parents because I finally saw what a healthy relationship looked like.

When my wounds were ripped open after marriage and children, my natural inclination was to fall into myself and not allow anyone to see the broken pieces of my heart or the damage I was causing to my husband and children. There was too much shame, pain, and confusion. How could I turn into a different person at thirty years old? Apparently, our wounds are waiting for the right time to be ripped open, and that is why I am writing this book. I want you to know that no matter when your wounds come open, you are seen and heard. There is someone in your life who has shown you kindness and cares for you. Do not shore up your walls and push people away. Allow light to come into your world. When we realize we are broken in ways that seem unimaginable, it can be difficult to face. We want to pretend we have everything together and can function normally. Well, life is full of unexpected twists and turns, and unpacking unforeseen baggage is one of them.

Whether you are 16, 25, 33, 48, or 65, it is never too late or too early to invite God into your story. Who in your life has been a reflection of His love and mercy? He works through the people in our lives to share His love. He doesn't want us to take the journey alone.

Life in community

Moving from a place of self-reliance to inclusivity can be a rather foreign experience. If you have only depended on yourself for a long time, then it can feel weird to start allowing others in your life, asking for help, and inviting people into your mess. My first step in this process was going to church.

I started reading the Bible because I longed to know God, but at that time, I had absolutely no interest in the mess within the four walls of a church. Then, I read a passage that changed my world. Romans 12:4-6 says, "For as in one body we have many members, and the members do not all have the same function, so we, though many, are one body in Christ, and individually members one of another. Having gifts that differ according to the grace given to us, let us use them." Right there in plain English (depending on your translation) God was calling me to live in community with other Christians.

I was furious, to say the least. There was no way I wanted to go back to the church world. I already had trust issues because of my dad, and after a bad Christian boyfriend experience, I was more than weary of men who called themselves believers. In fact, when I read I was supposed to be in community with other believers, I put my two cents in about it with God. I said, "Fine. You have said I am to be in community. And because I am a rule follower and I love You, I will. But I will not marry or date any man who calls himself a Christian. Christian men are not reliable, and I will never again enter a relationship with a man who goes to church on Sunday morning. I have more strength than they do, and I will not do that to myself again." Oh, friend. God has a sense of humor! Over the years, He saw I was serious. I would not date a guy who went to church on Sunday morning, but I also realized that I would not marry anyone who did not have a strong relationship with Christ.

Are you ready for this? Are you ready to hear part of my love story with our Father? My husband is a God-loving, Jesus-focused *Seventh Day Adventist*. What does that mean? He loves God and attends service on *Saturdays*. I hope you see God's hand in this because I laugh every time I think of it. Here was a Catholic-turned-non-denominational young woman handpicked for a Seventh Day Adventist. Historically, these two groups have not respected one another.

In our adulthood, my husband and I both found ourselves in relationship with Christ apart from the churches our families raised us in. Each of us has brought pieces of our faith upbringing to the marriage because we are very respectful of our parents' strong faith and the gifts they gave us through this faith. However, we do not attend our childhood churches.

So, as I listened to our Father and moved begrudgingly into community, I shared with Him my worries and doubts. And He listened. He knew my wounds were deep from my father's rejection and a young Christian man's actions. Our Father saw my pain and hurt. He listened to my wounds and loved me through them. As I entered community in obedience to Him, I still had my wall up concerning relationships, but He had a plan. He wanted me in community so that I would see Him in new ways as I engaged in life with other Christians. And I did.

As I navigated the scary corridors, literally, of the church world again, God was with me. He placed loving and accepting people in my path to come alongside me in moments of doubt and difficulty. God did not push me to re-enter painful relationships or tell me to change who I was and put my deepest hurts on display for others to judge or pontificate on. Instead, God wrapped me in His arms as I opened up and pulled down my walls. Because this process had to be on my terms and I did not invite Him in completely, I had some very dark years during that time. As I re-entered church community, I was hesitant about fully embracing it. I had been burned so badly the last time that I tiptoed into the world of believers, but God remained faithful.

Knowing our complexities and the ups and downs of the church world, why does God call us into community? Because He did not create us to live life on our own. Scripture says, "For just as each of us has one body with many members, and these members do not all have the same function, so in Christ we, though many, form one body, and each member belongs to all the others" (Romans 12:4-5 NIV). How cool is that? Your strength will complement mine, and neither of us has to do it on our own! Granted, community among believers does not always mean perfect harmony. There are tensions we must navigate when we live in community, but I encourage you to think of those situations in a new way.

When we enter into a relationship with God, inviting Him to walk alongside us, He gives us the ability to extend grace and understanding in new ways as He helps us deal with our wounds. If we remain in conversation with Him, we are able to discern our next steps with more clarity and authority. For example, He will help us recognize unhealthy situations and guide us as we remove ourselves from them. When this happens, He will give us the ability to finish out a commitment peacefully or to bow out gracefully. We can do so without hurtful words and without being concerned or worried about what others may think of us for changing our commitment. Can you imagine what it must feel like to be able to stop worrying about what others think of you? So exciting!

Not only can we learn discernment, find our worth, and draw our strength from our heavenly Father, but when we are in relationship with Him, we are also able to extend His compassion and mercy to others. There are bound to be difficult days, hard conversations, and unpleasant moments. He will help us respond to them with mercy, grace, and compassion so that we are able to remain committed to our relationships and our goals, while refusing to succumb to negativity. It takes a lot of practice to keep our eyes on our Father so that we can respond this way, but it is possible. And it gives us the ability to partner with people and not feel crushed when those people respond or act out of their flesh.

What do I mean by "acting out of their flesh?" I mean following selfish desires instead of God (e.g., manipulating people, misappropriating funds, spreading gossip, cheating on a spouse, etc.). When you have been burned by a church community because people acted out in their flesh, it is natural to want to walk away and disengage from that community. Witnessing people's shortcomings in a supposedly safe place is difficult to process. When those moments impact you, it is really hard to stay committed and connected because the place and people you have classified as different from the rest of the world have shown their humanity. You can feel let down, disillusioned, and betrayed. Understandably, it can be difficult for you to choose to remain connected and not turn to being self-reliant again. I want to encourage you to turn to God in those moments and refuse to allow the whispers of the world to influence your decision. Be patient with yourself and the people involved. Do not be the first one to cast a stone, which you may really want to do, or you will desire to be self-reliant again.

Whether you are single or raising a family, community is still critical to your connection with God. He wants to show you His love through inspired conversations, others' acts of kindness, and opportunities extended through ongoing fellowship. When difficult seasons come (and they will), rely on God. Seek His healing and love and allow Him to show you the way. Being part of a community does not mean you have to show up to church every Sunday and attend Bible study every week. God invites you to be part of His church, which is the body of Christ, and it lives inside of us. When we connect with other believers, the church is alive in that moment, whether it is a conversation in a parking lot, a fundraiser at a local park, or a gathering of people in a coffee shop. His church is not confined to four walls. During difficult seasons, I encourage you to seek His guidance in how to move forward and where to connect.

I have continued to work past my self-reliant nature by engaging in community and looking for one or two Christian women I could be myself with and not fear judgment. This continues to be my way of honoring Romans 12:4-6 because Scripture tells us that Jesus had an inner circle within the Apostles. It is not impossible to have close relationships with more than a few people, but it is difficult to sustain the depth of companionship critical for helping you navigate the seasons of great heartache and disappointment.

So, how will you choose to enter God's world and begin to allow others into your life?

Breaking lies

You can go at this life thing alone, choosing to believe it's better not to reach out to anyone for help or support. The lie I told myself was, "It's better not to reach out because then I won't be disappointed." That's when I lived life from a place of fear, rejection, and hurt. I believed it was better to rely on myself and not bother anyone else. The world promotes this attitude. Our culture encourages us to focus on ourselves and become self-reliant while it devalues the place and purpose of a friend and family support system. So, we give up and choose to forge ahead alone at the first sign of failure or rejection. I wonder what the world would look like if we approached the support system from a place of confidence and abundance? Instead of taking someone's cancellation, flaky response, or bad personality match as failure, we could look at it as a science experiment that didn't yield the results we expected. The situation didn't work out the way we hoped, so let's look for another opportunity with different variables.

When I first reentered the work force, I was terrified because there was no way I was going to find quality childcare for my children within my odd parameters. It took two years for me to wake up from my self-reliant methodology in parenting and finally, without a second thought, invite others in to be part of the journey. If they chose not to be a part of it, I would move on and find someone who was interested instead of shoring up my walls and not taking the chance for a bad match to happen. We fall into these thought patterns and reactions when we live from a place of pain and rejection. It's easier to bury the pain instead of facing the truth of why someone's lack of follow through or change in plans upsets us.

This approach to life is soul shatteringly wrong because it isolates us in our life rhythms. It has become too easy for some of us to shut out our family and friends. In fact, we can even become unable to connect with the family members under our own roof. We start to tell ourselves, "Since I'm doing all of this on my own, I might as well have my freedom, too. That would be much better." So, the real reason I believe God has called us into community is that we need one another to navigate this world. When we start to believe we can do it on our own, we begin believing our family is obsolete. We may not intentionally think this, but our actions will send that message. Instead of being vulnerable with our husbands and asking for assistance, we will believe they don't want to help us or that we are an inconvenience. Then, we will choose to do it on our own, which builds resentment. We will choose not to invite our children and family members into the mess because "we have it handled."

Sometimes we build up our defenses because we are tired of disappointment and want the task to be done the right way the first time, or we have asked for assistance in the past and have been let down. The truth is, no matter how close you are to God, the people around you will let you down. Then, why allow yourself to be close to God—the Father you can't see, feel, or touch? Simple. People are going to let you down whether you are close to God or not.

The ones in your life who love you the most will disappoint you, hurt your feelings, and fail to meet your expectations. How you respond to those situations and navigate through them is where God comes into the picture.

Have you ever disappointed someone and longed to make it better? God can help with that. Have you had a horrible experience but lacked the strength and confidence to walk away and not allow it to happen again? God's love and presence in your life make walking away and staying away possible. He wants to be with you in the disappointing moments and difficulties. He wants to show you the beauty of mercy and grace, which can appear in the disappointing moments of life. In fact, mercy and grace exist because of disappointments and letdowns.

When moments become excruciatingly painful, I like to imagine the walls in my home ten years from now. What pictures will be hanging on the wall? I dream of seeing pictures of my sister with her family and my husband and children throughout the years, with photos our parents and siblings scattered amongst them. We are blessed with several close family friends, and I imagine photos of them on the walls as well. In order to fill the wall with pictures, we must stop listening to the world's message that we can be self-reliant and go at life alone.

It can be very scary to hand over any part of your life to another person. I invite you to take a different first step. Share your current heartaches with your Father. He wants to sit with you and share in your story—all of it—the good, the bad, and the ugly. He will show you that He is not going anywhere. He will show you that trust is possible, and if someone in your life breaks it, He will heal you.

Each one of us is broken, and no matter how hard we work at being good and loving, we fail. In those moments God will pick us up and heal our wounds. When someone hurts us and tempts us to believe the lie of the world (that it is better to go at this alone and not reach out), God will heal us if we invite Him to do so.

What does it look like for God to heal you in this way? Well, first, He walks with you through the pain. He doesn't try to take it away. He understands it is there and you have to wrestle with it, sorting through the truth and the lies. He will talk with you about it as you try to understand the situation and what happened. As the pain starts to go away, which usually requires some time, He will help you take steps to move forward. For example, when my husband and I have said words each one of us regrets, God has helped us forgive and continue to communicate about our hopes and dreams. So, when your spouse or best friend says hurtful words and you find it difficult to trust and be open, ask God for help, comfort, and the ability to forgive. God *will* help. I have found inviting God into the pain and disappointment allows me to bounce back more quickly from hurt and anger.

It's a great relief not to be forced to rely on my own energy, love, and compassion in marriage and parenting. I used to take great pride in all I could accomplish, and, to be honest, I still do sometimes, but when hard days happen, I need God to help me push through with grace.

Journal Prompt

One of my greatest strengths is my independence. It
where I meet God regularly. I'm constantly learnin
which I push to forge life on my own, not allowing
provide assistance, or let me down. This is an area of
brings me the greatest joy and misery. I've learned to .gate it
differently and if this is an area you struggle with I hope these
prompts will help you to begin a journey of inviting others in,
knowing it won't be perfect.

1) What area in your life are you holding onto tightly?

2) How would your life change if you didn't feel alone?

3) Is there someone in your life you can turn to, confide in?

Prayer

Dear Lord, thank You for being part of my life and loving me
unconditionally. Please show me how to trust you. I long to discover
a transcendent peace in my life that will accompany me in any
situation. I am weary and exhausted. I don't want to continue
carrying the weight of the world. It is such a burden, and I am so
tired. Please come into my life, especially the critical places where I
desperately need Your love and grace. Amen.

6

God's Character as Our Father

Your love, Lord, reaches to the heavens,
your faithfulness to the skies. —Psalm 36:5 (NIV)

Sinners are seen

How would you feel if Jesus met you on one of your daily errands, like at the gas station or the grocery store, and told you about a gift He had for you? If you didn't recognize Him, you might think He was crazy and walk away. But if you stayed and listened to Him for a few minutes, the truth of His love would stun you.

This happened to a Samaritan woman once (see John 4). When she went to the well to get water for the day, the Lord choose to talk with her, and it stunned her. This woman had had five husbands and was currently living with a man who was not her husband. In other words, her track record left a little to be desired.

Why had she married been married to five men? When someone bounces from relationship to relationship, it usually indicates an internal struggle, an unsettled heart. Have you been inconsistent with relationships? Unable to fully commit either in romance or friendship? When we have a wound in us that has not healed, we are unable to live in a healthy, committed way. The wound can rip open and show itself in our behavior, words, and actions toward others.

Let's take a closer look at the woman at the well. We do not know how she lost her husbands. In biblical times, a man could divorce a woman by publicly saying, "I divorce you." If she was a promiscuous gal, it is very possible that the men chose to divorce her. Illness or warfare may also have claimed the life of one or more of her husbands. Regardless of the reasons, though, it was uncommon to have married five men, even in those uncertain times, and when she met Jesus, she was living a less than desirable life.

While our choices may not look like the Samaritan woman's, we have all had times in our lives when we can say, "Those actions are not what I want to be remembered by." We can all point to situations we wish we would have handled differently. There are many times in my past when the pain of rejection has overtaken my heart and I've lashed out in unspeakable ways. Our tongue is life or death, and we choose how to wield it. When there is pain and hurt in us that we are unwilling to acknowledge, we are liable to become destructive to those who come across our path. I wonder if this is why the Samaritan woman was married five times. Did she sabotage her relationships? Was her early life so difficult that she did not know any other way to live?

The truth is that the Samaritan woman was not in a peaceful place in her life. The Lord could see pain and hurt in her, and He spoke to that pain and hurt by giving her a gift. He told her true life can be experienced; she did not have to continue living as she had been.

I imagine the Samaritan woman's daily life was less than ideal. She would have been shunned for living with a man outside of marriage, so she must have struggled to find joy and purpose. Then, the Lord took the time to talk with her. He saw her wounds and her past and said, "If you knew the gift of God and who it is that asks you for a drink, you would have asked him and he would have given you living water" (John 4:10). Jesus didn't stop there, though. He revealed Himself as Messiah so that she would know who He was and could ask Him for "living water." He invited her into a new relationship—a new way of living and seeing the world. He didn't hold her past decisions against her. He didn't give conditions for her to receive His gift. It was her choice. If she chose to come to Him, she would never thirst again because He would be there to love and cherish her. If you choose to come to Him, He will be there for you, too.

Shame. Guilt. Uncertainty. These emotions usually hold me back from making an effort to form new relationships. I sometimes wonder what life looked like for the Samaritan woman after she accepted the Lord that day. Did she allow the Father to love her as no man ever had? Did she discover that He loved her with a protective love rivaled by no one? The Lord's promise was to give her life if she came to Him, and He promises you the same thing.

Will you choose to spend time with the Lord so that He may heal the wounds of your heart? Are you starting to discover the hurts lying beneath the surface?

Character introduced

One of the character traits of God is His willingness to open His arms up to us. The song "Forever Reign" speaks of our Father's love and how we are invited to run into His open, loving arms. There is no greater feeling than to be welcomed into an inviting place after we have been away for a long time. God is waiting for you to allow Him to embrace you. He longs to hear about your day, discuss the nuisances of work, and be the Father you never had.

Through His might, love, and grace, God can fill the crevices of you heart that have been laid open and left unfulfilled. He can heal your wounds and restore you to wholeness again. His love is so far-reaching that no person, thing, or circumstance can stand in its way. Even in the dark places, He is there. If you are in a situation of great devastation, if you find yourself back in a dark place, if you are overcome with grief, God is there with you. There is nowhere He cannot go and be.

God can heal the wounds of your past that have invaded your present. There is no reason you have to continue living as a victim. You are not the child who was rejected or abandoned. You are a daughter of Christ, and He loves you without apology. There are many great things He has in store for your life. Did you know that He knitted you, on purpose, in your mother's womb? There is no accidental piece of you. (See Psalm 139.) Through your brokenness, hurts, and pains, He can heal you and share His glory with others. You can live a life of joy and peace by having a relationship with God and allowing Him to be your Abba.

It is so easy for us to get in our own way, stay inside our own head, and doubt the love and grace that is waiting for us at our

Father's feet. Though we listen to what the world has said about us, hear the expectations of women in our culture, and conclude that we can't be good enough to measure up, the complete opposite is true.

Have you ever been uplifted with a kind word? Have you found delight in being seen by someone who smiled at you and asked how your day was? Well, that can happen every day. When you spend time with the Father, you are healed and transformed. You start to see Him in everyday life, and He intentionally reveals Himself there. He wants you to know He is watching over you, caring for you, loving you, and supporting you in the trenches of life. He does not want you to forget He is waiting to have conversations with you and seeking to be in community with you. He has great things planned for your life, but the only way you can discover what those things are is by spending time with Him. When we aren't spending time with Him, we can't see the opportunities He is providing us because we aren't listening—we have turned our ears and hearts off to His presence. This is like being in a drought in your marriage or work situation. When you don't feel connected, it's easy to feel left out and uncertain about what to say or do. The same is true with God.

When we aren't intentionally making time for Him, we tune Him out like a bad song on the radio.

God wants so much for you. He wants you to have energy and spirit to offer a smile that lifts others' spirits and makes their day. Because there is so much brokenness in this world, He wants His children to be beacons of light that overwhelm the earth and push back the darkness. This can only happen if you take the time to get to know Him and break down the walls of misunderstanding, untruths, and pain. When you are wounded by an earthly father, it is very difficult to want to get to know another one, especially if you can't see, feel, or touch Him. It is a scary leap of faith that leaves you vulnerable and full of conflicting emotions, but it is worth it.

If you desire to get to know your Father by sharing time with Him, you will need three things: a Bible, a pen, and paper. You don't have to rely on another person to make time for you to share your thoughts. You don't have to make sure your companion is a good fit for you. God already knows who you are, and the Bible is full of stories about people from every walk of life, from tax collectors to fishermen and from Paul, the converted Christian persecutor, to John the Baptizer.

As you spend time with the Lord, ask Him questions about being a father and what that looks like. Don't be afraid to have a blunt conversation with Him. I encourage you to ask, "Why did this happen to me as a child?" I also strongly encourage you not to live in those conversations for too long. In order to grow and live into the purpose He has for you, you must take action and clear out the baggage on your doorstep. But do not be fearful of asking Him the hard questions. He knows you have them, and they are necessary for you to discover the truth of His love. He will not smite you for asking tough questions, sharing your feelings, and expressing the doubts and hurts in your heart. In case you haven't guessed already, He knows they are there. He wants to heal them, He wants to spend time with His daughter and talk to her; He wants to be the rock she can rely on through all things.

Here's a pretty cool thing about God: He doesn't invade our privacy. If you're wondering why He hasn't healed you yet if He's so powerful, it is because our Heavenly Father is not going to intrude on your privacy and take away what you have not asked Him to take. Your heart, mind, and soul are yours, and He waits to be invited into those personal places. He waits to hear, "Hi."

He is all powerful, and you are His daughter, but He respects your choice and waits for you, eagerly hoping you will choose Him.

God longs to share the glories of His creation with you. He wants to be there to reveal the beauty in this world He has created for you. He wants to be part of your earthly journey and delight in your accomplishments, hold you when there is difficulty, and provide the wisdom and insight you will need to step through this broken world and live out His purpose for you. What He has for you is greater than anything you can imagine. This truth can sometimes be hard to believe. My acceptance of it often depends on my mood. Oddly enough, every time I pause and get out of my own way, I see the enormity of God's gifts in my life. Whether or not you accept this truth about your own life is entirely up to you. I just want you to know God has joys and delights for you that are beyond comprehension.

Relationship details

What does it look like to be Abba's daughter? Are there strings attached?

Discovering the intricacies of a father-daughter relationship with God can be overwhelming and, at times, daunting and surreal. Is there really a God who cares about how we feel each day and the decisions we make for ourselves? If we have been alone for a while, this can seem unlikely. We become accustomed to a certain way of living, a certain way of looking at the world. The possibility of something better is intriguing yet unreal.

In this chapter I want to unpack what it looks like to have a relationship with God the Father. Entering into a new relationship with someone is nerve-racking, and when that someone is the Creator of the universe (whom you are not able to see and touch), it makes things even more complicated. The first step is learning who God really is, not relying on perceptions from our childhood or statements made by friends, society, or the media. Some of those outside influences might originate with well-meaning people (like this book for instance), but the thoughts and opinions of these people should bear only a certain amount of weight. God wants you to engage personally with Him so that He can directly impact your heart and soul as you seek Him out. A new confidence will arise in you as you engage His Word with the help of the Holy Spirit, Who will begin conforming your personal thoughts and ideas to God's truth. This kind of engagement has the power to steer you during difficult situations and uncertainties.

Once you have decided to enter into a personal relationship with God, the next step is to begin spending time with Him. This is easier said than done. It may take years or decades to get to a point where you naturally make time for the Creator you can't see. I have difficulty making intentional time for my mom, and she is a living, breathing human being. Instead of beating yourself up when you notice it has been awhile since you spent time with God, take a moment to say, "Hi. I know you're there, but it's been awhile. How are you?" If those aren't the words you use to greet a loved one, then replace my sentence with one you would use.

In the early stages of building my relationship with God, the key for me was to show up consistently. Think of it like dating. In the beginning, you are excited to spend time with this new and fascinating person. You move heaven and earth to make time for each other, to go places together, and to stay up late talking on the phone (wait, that was my generation—now you stay up late texting or skyping). At some point the magic fizzles out, and instead of coming up with creative dates to impress each other, you end up sitting on the couch watching a movie. After marriage, you begin to rely on everyday chores to replace conversation, and you watch mindless television shows together to relax and rejuvenate. Something similar can happen in our relationship with our Father. It might be happening right now for you, or maybe it has been happening for some time. Regardless, it *is* normal. Instead of feeling guilty because you haven't spent enough time with Him lately, take that thought and turn it into, "Hello, Abba." He desires for you to seek Him out and come to know Him.

Here's the neat part: He encourages us to take one step at a time. We do not have to figure everything out right away. The other encouraging part is that He knows we will falter, mess up, and NEVER EVER have it perfect. Also, as we navigate this new relationship, He will bring people into our lives to encourage us and support us during the transition.

Unending healing

God's fatherly love for us is a complex facet of His character. That love draws us closer to Him and inspires us to live lives that honor Him. Being a child of God does come with a few perks: life after death, an everlasting love, and full acceptance. Much of the time, we want to focus on what we get out of our relationship with Him—how it is going to benefit us and what we will receive from it. When we do this, we fail to truly understand God's fatherly love.

Have you ever been in a fight with your spouse or a friend and all you can think about is how this person wronged you, what he or she should have done differently, and how he or she should change in the future? As children of God, we can be tempted to have the same attitude toward our heavenly Father, asking what He has done for us lately or wondering why He didn't cause the wonderful thing we prayed for to happen. When we view our relationship with Him from this perspective, we are unable to take a broader view of our circumstances and to understand the dynamics of a true relationship.

God disciplines us—not with fire and brimstone discipline, even though a lot of those moments occurred in the Old Testament, but with a parental kind of discipline. Because we are His children who are clothed in the righteousness of His Son, His discipline is paired with mercy. Proverbs 3:12 (NIV) assures us, "…the Lord disciplines those he loves, as a father the son he delights in."

In Psalm 51 we see the results of this kind of discipline in a difficult Father-son moment. David wrote this confessional psalm to his Father after committing great sin. The words show that David's heart has been softened by the Lord's discipline. David asks for forgiveness, knowing he will receive it because the Lord will not "despise" a "broken spirit" and a "contrite heart" (Psalm 51:17 NIV). On the contrary, the Lord can work in a softened heart and broken spirit to transform that person's character, and David knew this. He asked God to "create in [him] a pure heart" (Psalm 51:10 NIV), knowing that God would do so.

While God will forgive and cleanse us when we sin, He will not erase the consequences of our earthly decisions. As any parent knows, children learn from consequences. However, when we have truly repentant hearts, God's discipline will be tempered with mercy, and He will cleanse and forgive us, removing our sin from us "as far as the east is from the west" (Psalm 103:12 NIV), just as He did for David.

What does this mean? Even when you mess up, God loves you. And I'm not talking about spilled milk kind of mess ups; I'm talking about grave injustices. David saw a woman he desired, killed her husband, and took her as his own. God still forgave and cleansed him. So, no matter what sins you have committed, your Father will welcome you with open arms. If you have a truly repentant heart, He will discipline you with mercy. God has shown all of us great mercy through His Son's sacrifice. All our sins are forgiven, even the ones we hold deep inside and will not allow anyone to see for fear of rejection.

Journal Prompt

Each of us has a unique relationship with God. Take some time and think about your relationship with Him. If you don't have one, I hope these journal prompts will be your first step in exploring the opportunity.

1) What truths do you know about God?

2) In this moment, today, God is _____.

3) How would it change your life to have a safe place to turn to in any situation?

Prayer

Dear Father, thank you for extending the invitation to me for a loving relationship. Would You show me how to be vulnerable and receive Your gifts? Looking for You in my daily life can be difficult. I confess I don't always do that, but I would like to. I want to know You more and discover healing and strength, even in the difficult moments. Please continue to put people in my path who will show me Your character and teach me more of who You are and how I can get to know You. Amen.

7

Redefine Love

**Give thanks to the Lord, for he is good;
his love endures forever. —1 Chronicles 16:34 (NIV)**

No matter what we tell ourselves, sometimes we hear these whispers: "If I had been better, maybe he would have loved me. If I had tried harder, the gaping hole in my heart wouldn't be there. If I had been... then he would be...."

When there is an absence of unconditional love in our lives, we begin to perceive love as a conditional commodity, like so much else in our world. After all, we live in a transactional world, where you trade money for goods and work to receive a certain amount of compensation. We can identify give and take when we look at jobs, homes, and education. In other areas, like sports, music, and art, a certain level of natural talent is required to be successful, and then progress is achieved through measurable effort. These are regular, observable facts of life. If we want to achieve a goal, then we must do a certain amount of work in return, and even after all that work and effort, we can still fall short of success.

Does this picture look familiar to you? Would you agree this is how we are raised to function in our world? We are programmed to perform for our teachers and bosses, to be a good example for those around us, and to be high achievers in order to succeed. With this model for success and achievement ingrained in us from birth, it isn't any wonder we often transfer the same model to relationships. We start performing in order to be accepted by those around us. We act a certain way in relationships to please the other person and keep them with us. These are not inherently bad responses in a relationship, but when we lose our identity and stifle our personalities in order to be accepted and pleasing to others, damage occurs. Often without realizing it, we become timid in sharing our thoughts and opinions and in trying new things.

If we don't think we can offer what the transactional model requires for success, we often embrace the opposite extreme. Instead of adapting to those around us and losing our identity in relationships, we can rebel and refuse to let people in, erecting emotional walls to prevent them from hurting or influencing us.

We were not designed to be enslaved to either extreme, however. Instead, we were created to embrace ourselves completely in every relationship and situation. We were never meant to be the same person in each interaction. We were designed to be conformed to the image of Christ (see Romans 8:29) and to be a unique reflection of Him to others. This requires us to look at each of our relationships individually, giving what is needed to each one. Sometimes we will need to step up and lead, and other times, we will need to listen and be supportive. We are called to bring the love of Christ to each situation, and in all of it, we are always called to be ourselves—not hiding who we are or stifling the words we feel called to share. Likewise, we need to allow others to be themselves and share, too, and when we are not open to their thoughts, we should stop and ask ourselves if we are around the right people or if our defenses are so high that we are not allowing anyone in.

We have beauty within us to be shared with others, not stifled by the world. And we are not to stifle someone else's beauty; instead, we are to lift each other up. We have been designed to complement one another and build on each other's strengths.

How do we live this way? How do we learn to embrace the entirety of who we are and engage in relationships without fear of rejection? How do we fully and graciously accept who other people are? How do we keep from reverting to the habit of adapting to those around us out of fear or defensiveness?

None of us sets out to engage in relationships with a transactional mindset, but in the fast-paced, expectant world we live in today, it is hard not to look at relationships and love this way. This perception seems to occur on an almost subconscious level. Why wouldn't we equate love to a conditional situation when every other aspect of our lives seems to be part of a balanced equation?

How would you like to rewrite this reality and replace it with truth? The love our earthly fathers modeled lacked the unconditional element, so it left us confused and uncertain. As women who have felt deep rejection, how do we change our norms? Since you are reading this book, you are likely trying to navigate those wounds and discover a different way of experiencing the world. You are dissatisfied with either your relationships or your responses to others—perhaps a little of both. When there is an absence of unconditional love in your life, it is difficult to know how to interact with people in a healthy manner.

However, it is possible to experience unconditional love and apply it to the world around you, even if you have never received it from one of the two people who contributed to your very existence.

No strings attached

If you stopped and looked at the relationships in your life, could you honestly say they are full of unconditional love? When I looked closely at my relationships, I discovered I was equating my performance as a wife, daughter, and mother with the amount of love I deserve. By the grace of God, these lies are being broken, and I'm discovering the truth of unconditional love. However, this is taking time and constant communication with our Father.

The song "The God I Know" clearly illustrates God's unconditional love for us. I wish I could sing it for you because the words are so pure and true. God expects nothing from you in exchange for His love. He has no hidden agenda. He created you with delight, and He wants to be with you in all your moods and moments—the good, the bad, and the ugly. He already loves you unconditionally. He offers the love you have yearned for since your first rejection.

While the world around you is constantly demanding something from you in exchange for basic acceptance, God offers you His unending love with no strings attached. If you have ever been in a dysfunctional relationship, this concept is probably foreign to you, so let's take a moment and unpack this truth a little bit more.

Does God really love with no strings attached? Is there a hidden catch that will become apparent once the relationship is underway? No. There is no loophole, no catch. You might wonder how this is possible and how you can be certain this is the absolute truth. I won't lie to you; accepting God's love does take faith. There will be moments (or days or years) when you wonder if He has abandoned you or if He is not listening, but before you allow this to discourage you, let me ask you—have you ever experienced similar moments with a close friend or your husband? I know I have, and it takes communication and quality time together for me to realize that my friend or husband is truly there for me. The same is true with God.

Being in a relationship with Him requires intentionality on our part to seek Him, listen to His words, and invite Him into our lives—just as we would a friend or partner.

Take a moment and imagine. What would it be like for you to know a Father who loves you unconditionally? He will wrap you in His arms when days are hard and hold your hand when weeping racks your body. There will be no more isolation or feelings of abandonment. You will receive encouragement and guidance when you seek it, and you will always be understood. As you navigate human relationships in a new way, He will be right beside you to guide and protect you. When you make a mistake, He will pick you up, hold you close, and continue the journey alongside you. And His love will change you. You will discover an ability to love others unconditionally.

I want to share a little secret with you that I wish I had known when I started this venture with God. Even though I have experienced His unconditional love for years, I still mess up and act out in horrible ways because I'm human. None of us can live every moment perfectly. Our sinful nature will dominate some of our moments and squash all the good we thought we were creating. (I hope this little secret brings a sigh of relief to those of you who are perfectionists and provides a strong dose of encouragement to those of you who are not.)

Since we live in a broken world, I don't believe any of us can eliminate our shortcomings. God knows we are going to sin and make poor decisions. We are going to have moments we wish we could swipe from everyone's memories and rewrite. Through experience I can promise you that God is still waiting to hold you in His arms and love you unconditionally.

Discover your gift

God does not say, "You must do this and this in order for me to love you." If you believe He does, then you have believed a lie. Depending on the messages you received as a child, that lie may be planted deep in your subconscious. Maybe you don't even entertain the idea of earning God's love because you have believed the lie that God doesn't love you at all. When we choose to get to know God and discover His unconditional love, we must learn to fight continually against these lies.

If we haven't experienced unconditional love for years (or decades), how do we begin to discover this gift from our Creator? One of the first steps is to spend time with Him. We cannot build trust and understanding with anyone if we don't take time to be with that person. We especially need to take time with our heavenly Father, whom we cannot see or touch. Even though His creation and goodness surround us, it can be quite difficult for us at the beginning of our journey to understand how to go about spending time with Him.

There are countless Christians who suffer from the wounds of their earthly fathers yet do not know the love of our heavenly Father. They do not know what it is like to truly have a personal relationship with God. Maybe they have not put time and energy into building a relationship with Him, or maybe they don't even know a relationship with Him is possible. They might even be going through a difficult season in their faith.

If you are going through a difficult season, I want you to know it is normal to question your faith, your walk with God, and your relationship with Him. He expects it. What He wants is for you to talk to Him about your questions, even during the difficult times. Even if you are unsure of His existence, say "hello" every week. Tell Him about your day; keep the lines of communication open. If you seek Him, you will find Him. He will reveal His presence to you, and then, you will find yourself continuing to seek Him out in the good times and the bad.

No matter what we do, God will still love us and stand by us. When we come to Him with a true desire to know Him and be with Him, He will not abandon us. There are no hidden strings; He loves us. Our Father wants to be part of our lives, even in the dark places.

One story I know continues to show me the truth of God's unconditional love. It is about a man who had the whole world at his fingertips and was given every luxury available. He had beautiful women, plentiful food, and the challenges of a high-profile job. He had worked hard to achieve his success and was reaping the fruits of his labor. How could he want for anything?

This man was David. There are books written about him and the glory he brought to the nation of Israel after God ordered his anointing as king. But, as I noted earlier, David made the horrific decision to kill a man after committing adultery with that man's wife. This sin should have cast David out of favor with the Lord forever, but, even though God did not shield David from the consequences of his sin, the Lord never ceased to love him. And if God could love David after such actions, then He can love us, too. No matter what sins we have committed in the past, God's love is not out of reach because God's love truly is unconditional. It can be difficult to wrap our heads around this truth.

While we don't know David's mental state at the time of his actions, we do know that after he rose to greatness, he stopped relying on the Lord and spending time with Him. David had become self-reliant and no longer felt that he needed the Lord's constant guidance and protection. He allowed the world to influence his decisions, and he conformed to others' expectations, which was very far from what the Lord had called him to do and be.

When David went to the Lord and repented, he was not turned away. God did not reject His son. Can you imagine committing a grave sin and not being rejected? Again, this is the story I turn to when I have sinned against my loved ones, neglected my time with the Lord, and allowed the world's messages to mute the truth of God in my mind and heart. This story shows us that we should never hide from God. Even when we have lost our way, He wants to be with us. His unconditional love is waiting for us.

You may be wondering, "Ok. So, David was welcomed into God's arms, and that was that? How is that okay?" Well, that's not the entire story. God did accept David into His arms and showered him with unconditional love, which is what our souls long for. But God did not shield David from the consequences of his sin. The child David conceived in adultery with Bathsheba died at birth, and David did not receive all the blessings intended for his reign. Instead, God said David's son Solomon would experience those blessings as long as Solomon loved the Lord with all his heart.

Let's unpack these truths for a moment because there is healing in knowing the truth. David committed murder. In most families this act would be unforgiveable. The murderer would be cast out and shunned, even if he repented of his actions. In God's family, however, a murderer with a repentant heart is never cast out. That means no matter what actions we have taken, God will still love and forgive us. There are open arms ready to receive us despite our lies, hurtful words, and selfish manipulations. He will always show us mercy and grace.

The story of David shows us that unconditional love and the Lord's blessings are two different things, and this is GOOD news. When we mess up and our lives are not what we wish for them to be, God will still love us unconditionally. He will not withhold His love because we are full of rage, manipulation, and selfishness. However, He will not bless our lives when we are living from those places, and therein lies a big truth we often miss.

We believe that if we are not receiving blessings, seeing good things happen, and getting what we pray for, then God does not love us. Unconditional love does not work like that. God loves you no matter what is going on in your world. He loves you if you are cheating on your boyfriend or hating everyone in your life. He loves you if you are cutting yourself to hide the pain or disengaging from the world because it hurts too much to interact with others.

The reason this truth is so powerful is there is nothing, absolutely nothing, we can do to earn or lose God's love. We cannot act a certain way to earn His love. We cannot dress a certain way to earn His love. We cannot treat people a certain way to earn His love. There is no magical formula that makes the Lord love us. He loves us no matter what choices we make.

We are programmed in a world where actions result in an outcome, but God's love goes beyond those parameters.

His love does not have boundaries and will supersede any limitations you try to put on it. The good news is there is nothing you have done in the past that will keep you away from His love. There is nothing you will do in the future that can eliminate His love for you. God's love is waiting for you and will always be there for you to receive.

When we are walking in relationship with the Lord and engaged in daily interactions with Him, we can start to see the blessings He has for us because our eyes and hearts are open to them. This is not a manipulation; it is a normal dynamic in relationships. For example, it is difficult to care for a friend if you do not talk to one another. It is nearly impossible to love and care for your partner if you two do not speak to one another for weeks on end. Are you able to give your partner loving words more easily when you both have been spending time together and communicating regularly or when life has pulled you in different directions?

In my marriage I'm able to see Kurt's acts of kindness and tenderness when we have spent time engaged with one another and not as two ships passing in the night. The same is true for the Lord. I can see His presence and blessings in my life when I am giving Him my time and inviting Him into my mess. That means I go to Him in the bad times as well as the good ones. It means ending up on my knees in prayer to Him after I've had a fight with my children or submitting to Him in defeat after I have tried and failed again to be a loving friend.

A new world

Discovering the truth of God's unconditional love will change your life. You will see the world in a new way, and great healing will take place. When you rely on a dependable source for love, encouragement, and contentment, you can function from a new place. Instead of looking to those around you for love, courage, and affirmation, you will begin to rely on the one true Father for a steady stream of unconditional love. It is an ever-flowing stream of love, waiting for you to drink of it. The water from this river is life-giving, refreshing, and even more joy-inducing than the "butterflies" you get when you first fall in love! This stream will sustain you in the darkness and never run dry.

What would your relationships look like if your wounds of rejection were healed? What would your world look like if you placed your insecurities in the safe hands of a loving Father?

There is an epidemic of "victim" mentality. We are blaming others for our lack of follow through, our inability to take responsibility for our actions, and our failure to become the people we were created to be. For some of us, the insecurity is rooted in our father's rejection and cripples us from being able to move forward in our lives the way we wish. We are so caught up in the world around us that we do not stop to look within and take stock of our role and responsibility in the situations unfolding around us. Knowing my walk and witnessing the walks others, I think some of us navigate the world from this place due to a fear of rejection. We worry about what others will think, and we don't move forward because things may not turn out the way we hoped. All these fears and concerns are normal. And guess what? Fear will always be with us. When we live a life engaged with others and trying new things, there will always be some level of fear. It is how we channel the fear that can free us from the victim mentality.

Imagine moving forward in fear, confidently knowing you are loved no matter the result. Your actions and efforts do not impact the way you are loved. Even if you fail, you are loved. Even if you lose your cool and go off on someone, you are loved. What if you faced the world from a place knowing you are cherished, seen, and valued?

The world would change if all the daughters of Christ took each step in life knowing His unconditional love. On the hard days, you would know you are loved. As you tackled difficult projects, you would know you are accepted and seen. If you lost your cool and blew up, you would feel healing and love immediately because you took it to the Father and said, "I messed up. Please be with me. I need you. Please come alongside me." Instead of living in the guilt and shame, you would be able to forgive yourself and allow the love of our Father to wash over you.

Imagine that after a failure, you were able to sit with someone who would listen to all the ins and outs, understand your perspective, and lovingly speak into your situation in the way you most needed.

What would that do to your world? What if instead of beating yourself up for weeks (or even months), you were able to release your failure and, after a really big hug, reflect on the situation objectively? What if you could learn something from your failure that you could use in the future, like how to navigate the situation better or develop better boundaries?

Now, imagine what your family would be like. How would your family look if after a big fight, you and your husband were able to take your hurts to the Lord and be healed? What if you and your husband could look at one another and know each of you has the other's best interest at heart? You could rewrite the story of your marriage. Your children would see a new script taking place.

How would knowing unconditional love impact your work environment? Would you be able to communicate in a healthy way with your co-workers? Would you be able to stand up to someone who continually walks all over you? Would you be able to let your walls down and see those around you in their vulnerability?

When we live from a place of unconditional love, we are able to be more empathetic without being a doormat. We are able to listen to the hurts and wounds of those around us and care for them without judgment. We are able to meet people where they are in their walks. Each one of us is a daughter or son of God, but not all of us know it yet, and that is okay. No two journeys are meant to the be the same. So, imagine living without the desire to impress those around you. What would it be like to know someone adores you and there will never be rejection—only acceptance? Would this truth give you the confidence to be the person you were created to be?

I believe we all want to live a life without judgment—a life we will be proud to have lived. We are only on this earth for a finite period of time. How do we live well? And how do we do that without sacrificing our identities? The answer is we enter into a relationship with our true Father, who will show us the life He has intended for us. He will reveal the blessings He has in store for our future.

How do we discover this unconditional love?

Knowing God does not necessarily mean we have accepted His unconditional love. We may still be operating from a place of self-preservation; our walls could still be up. To find out if this is so, we make the choice to seek God. It can be in the small quiet moments of your day. Or in the tumultuous, heart wrenching minutes and hours of life. Your choice. All of this is your choice. And time and time again when I have chosen to say "hi" and share my ups and downs, He has shown up. Through my experience He will show us the way.

Journal Prompt

Inviting our Father to share in your life is the first step to experiencing His unconditional love. As you get to know Him and spend time journeying with Him through life, you will reach a point when you are ready to accept His unconditional love. To help you discover where you are in the journey, the prompts below are reflective in nature.

1) How do your most intimate relationships make you feel? (Examples of intimate relationships: immediate family, partner, close friendships.)

2) Is there a passion inside that you're afraid to share with those around you?

3) Are you ashamed of the person you were in the past? Are you in the process of healing from previous poor choices?

4) What are the five emotions you experience the most during the day?

5) How do you want people to remember you after you spend time with them?

Prayer

Dear Father, thank You for the gift of unconditional love. Thank You for loving me so much that You sent Your Son to die on a cross for my sins. Thank You for showering me with mercy and grace. Please show me how to treat those around me well and reveal the ways in which I can honor You. Please guide me in relationships and how to navigate the complexities of everyday interactions. I long to live life knowing I am covered in Your unconditional love, and it is a hard transition to make. Please bring encouragement and light into my life as I rewrite my future and include You in every step. Amen.

End Note

Up to you now

A relationship with God is in your hands. How often you want to see your Father and spend time with Him is up to you. There is no more hoping and wishing for a father who will send a birthday card or change his mind about wanting to be around you. Your Abba is ready when you are, waiting in great anticipation to hear your thoughts, ideas, and dreams. He will never reject you or leave you. He will never say, "Well, here's the thing. I just don't know how to be a dad, and I'm not interested in learning." The Lord God created you. Before you were even conceived, He was dreaming of your heart, the joys you would bring to the world, the way you would laugh, and how you would share the world around you with the people in your life. God loves you—completely.

No more waiting for Dad to show up and love you.

I have so much good news for you. No matter what you have done in the past, you are forgiven. No matter what you have done, God delights in you and has made you worthy. NO MATTER what choices you have made, how many people you have hurt, or how much guilt or shame is consuming you in this moment, YOU. ARE. LOVED. You are loved with a greatness beyond comprehension. You are loved with a fierceness unrivaled. You are delighted in like no other human on this planet.

Your past will only define you if you allow it. You have permission to release the burden. When you are hurt to your core, there are pieces of baggage and scars waiting to be reopened. Sometimes you don't even realize they are there until someone crosses you or pushes you too far, and you snap. Maybe you lash out after stress upon stress upon stress. Maybe you turn to hurting yourself because the physical pain overshadows your emotional turmoil.

Whatever you have done, you are loved. You are seen. And you can choose your future. You can rewrite the script you have been living out.

Our Father cares about your future and wants to make a way for you. It is your choice.

ABOUT THE AUTHOR

Trish Russell lives in the Midwest with her husband and three children. She continuously shares her recovery journey with the purpose of sharing hope and light to the far reaches of the world. You can learn more about her at www.commitandreclaim.com and become a member of her community where she spends time helping others commit and reclaim their life after trauma. Hearing from readers is one of her favorite joys so please send a note. If she doesn't respond right away, then she's off slaying dragons and hosting tea parties with her kiddos, and she'll respond as soon as she returns.

Made in the USA
Middletown, DE
01 April 2018